New Accents

General Editor: TERENCE HAWKES

S[

D0063329

IN THE SAME SERIES

MAURICE CHARNEY

SEXUAL FICTION

METHUEN
LONDON AND NEW YORK

First published in 1981 by
Methuen & Co. Ltd
11 New Fetter Lane, London EC4P 4EE
Published in the USA by
Methuen & Co.
in association with Methuen, Inc.
733 Third Avenue, New York, NY 10017

© *1981 Maurice Charney*

Printed in the United States of America

British Library Cataloguing in Publication Data

Charney, Maurice
Sexual fiction. — (New accents)
1. Sex in literature
I. Title   II. Series
808.83'9'353   PN3352.S5/

ISBN 0-416-31930-0
ISBN 0-416-31940-8 Pbk

For H.K.

'For she koude of that art the olde daunce.'

CONTENTS

GENERAL EDITOR'S PREFACE

IT is easy to see that we are living in a time of rapid and radical social change. It is much less easy to grasp the fact that such change will inevitably affect the nature of those academic disciplines that both reflect our society and help to shape it.

Yet this is nowhere more apparent than in the central field of what may, in general terms, be called literary studies. Here, among large numbers of students at all levels of education, the erosion of the assumptions and presuppositions that support the literary disciplines in their conventional form has proved fundamental. Modes and categories inherited from the past no longer seem to fit the reality experienced by a new generation.

New Accents is intended as a positive response to the initiative offered by such a situation. Each volume in the series will seek to encourage rather than resist the process of change, to stretch rather than reinforce the boundaries that currently define literature and its academic study.

Some important areas of interest immediately present themselves. In various parts of the world, new methods of analysis have been developed whose conclusions reveal the limitations of the Anglo-American outlook we inherit. New concepts of literary forms and modes have been proposed; new notions of the nature of literature itself, and of how it communicates, are current; new views of literature's role in relation to society flourish. *New Accents* will aim to expound and comment upon the most notable of these.

In the broad field of the study of human communication, more and more emphasis has been placed upon the nature and function of the new electronic media. *New Accents* will try to identify and discuss the challenge these offer to our traditional modes of critical response.

The same interest in communication suggests that the series should also concern itself with those wider anthropological and sociological areas of investigation which have begun to involve scrutiny of the nature of art itself and of its relation to our whole way of life. And this will ultimately require attention to be focused on some of those activities which in our society have hitherto been excluded from the prestigious realms of Culture. The disturbing realignment of values involved and the disconcerting nature of the pressures that work to bring it about both constitute areas that *New Accents* will seek to explore.

Finally, as its title suggests, one aspect of *New Accents* will be firmly located in contemporary approaches to language, and a continuing concern of the series will be to examine the extent to which relevant branches of linguistic studies can illuminate specific literary areas. The volumes with this particular interest will nevertheless presume no prior technical knowledge on the part of their readers, and will aim to rehearse the linguistics appropriate to the matter in hand, rather than to embark on general theoretical matters.

Each volume in the series will attempt an objective exposition of significant developments in its field up to the present as well as an account of its author's own views of the matter. Each will culminate in an informative bibliography as a guide to further study. And while each will be primarily concerned with matters relevant to its own specific interests, we can hope that a kind of conversation will be heard to develop between them: one whose accents may perhaps suggest the distinctive discourse of the future.

TERENCE HAWKES

ACKNOWLEDGEMENTS

B EHIND this book lies a course I have been giving at Rutgers University in sexual fiction, and I am grateful to my students for their unacknowledged collaboration. Their letters, questions and healthy skepticism deepened my understanding of the subject and helped to define what is really important. Some of the arbitrary pairings in the book – Miller and Lawrence, Roth and Jong, *My Secret Life* and *Fanny Hill* – come out of the course and are intended to make the books mutually illuminating. I must apologize in advance for dealing with important works of sexual literature apart from the authors' general careers, especially in the case of Henry Miller and D. H. Lawrence, although I would also have liked to go further in speaking about the careers of Roth and Nabokov. Part of the purpose of the present book is to argue for the existence of sexual fiction as an identifiable genre in its own right, so that the discussion must necessarily focus on books with an overtly sexual subject matter.

I acknowledge a special debt to the psychiatrist, Irving Schneider, who first interested me in the subject by a talk he gave on movies at the American Civilization seminar of Columbia University. I also learned a good deal from Karl Beckson when we were working together on an erotic literature anthology. Ann Snitow of Livingston College, who is an expert on sexual fiction in her own right, read the manuscript and offered valuable comments. My colleagues, George Kearns and Carol McGuirk, have been concerned with my further education. Abe Krash helped me with some of the legal implications of books that are unabashedly sexual and literary at the same time. Of my neighbors in Truro and Wellfleet, Norris Fliegel produced a copy of *Candy* at exactly the right moment, and Harry Levin generously supplied bibliographical references. My research assistant at Rutgers, Mark Gallaher, has expertly seconded my endeavors. Parts of Chapter 7 were delivered as a public lecture at the College of William and Mary. The lively students of the residence program and my hosts, Carlyle Beyer and Mathew Winston, made that a memorable occasion.

The bibliography at the end is not intended to be exhaustive, but to serve rather as a guide to a wide variety of materials relevant to the subject. I have generally quoted from easily available paperback editions of the basic texts (which may be found in the bibliography, as may articles and books cited), with page numbers after each quotation. For *My Secret Life*, I have quoted from the abridged edition, but recommend the formidable unabridged edition for further reading.

INTRODUCTION

W HEN asked to distinguish between pornography and eroticism, Alain Robbe-Grillet, the leading practitioner of the French New Novel, is reported to have said: 'Pornography is the eroticism of others' ('La pornographie, c'est l'érotisme des autres'). This nicely engages the verbal philandering about sexual words. One person's curiosa are another's dirty books, and, as Ned Polsky points out in his important essay, 'On the sociology of pornography', 'pornography' has meaning only in relation to the criteria of social class. There is no intrinsic reason why the courts should privilege middle-class pornography by such code phrases as 'redeeming social value' and 'community standards' while attacking the more raucous and cruder pornography of the non-cultivated classes. How can we justify special standards for books that do not apply to other forms of entertainment? The British Obscene Publications Act of 1959 at least admits that a book may be both obscene and have literary merit.

D. H. Lawrence tries valiantly to define pornography in his essay, 'Pornography and obscenity' (1929), reprinted in *Sex, Literature, and Censorship*. For Lawrence, pornography is always secret and suppressed; it is 'almost always underworld, it doesn't come into the open' (p. 69). And it debases healthy and natural sexual impulses:

> Pornography is the attempt to insult sex, to do dirt on it. This is unpardonable. Take the very lowest instance, the

picture post-card sold underhand, by the underworld, in most cities. What I have seen of them have been of an ugliness to make you cry. The insult to the human body, the insult to a vital human relationship! Ugly and cheap they make the human nudity, ugly and degraded they make the sexual act, trivial and cheap and nasty. (p. 69)

One could protest that Lawrence's sanitized and pornography-less sex is sex without demonic energy. In most sexual writing, secrecy is a necessary stimulus to the erotic imagination. Lawrence hardly offers a logical definition at all, since he uses 'pornography' as a dirty word. In this book I have avoided fine distinctions between terms such as 'pornographic', 'obscene', 'sexual' and 'erotic', because all these words are more or less synonymous, depending on the value judgments and class orientation of individual users. Lawrence's argument about pornography is thoroughly circular, as is the Kronhausens' attempt, in *Pornography and the Law*, to distinguish between erotic realism and pornography. Their lengthy effort is almost completely ornamental, and, as in Lawrence, we end with the same preconceptions with which we began.

The Other Victorians, a highly original exploration of Victorian sexuality by Steven Marcus, also belabors the distinction between pornography and literature. In his conclusion he sums up arguments he has been making throughout the book to prove that 'pornography is not literature':

First, there is the matter of form. Most works of literature have a beginning, a middle, and an end. Most works of pornography do not. A typical piece of pornographic fiction will usually have some kind of crude excuse for a beginning, but, having once begun, it goes on and on and ends nowhere. This impulse or compulsion to repeat, to repeat endlessly, is one of pornography's most striking qualities. (pp. 281–2)

Even if one accepts Marcus's rigid dichotomy, he is still hopelessly mired in words. On this basis we may say that

whatever sexual fiction has a beginning, middle and end –
like *Lady Chatterley's Lover* and *Story of O* – is therefore not
pornographic. I object strongly to Marcus's use of 'pornography' to describe bad sexual fiction. If the writing is good,
and therefore by Marcus's argument literature, it cannot
also be pornography. This completely begs the real question
of defining sexual fiction.

Marcus makes additional stipulations about the adverse
relation of pornography to literature. In terms of language,
for example:

> Although a pornographic work of fiction is by necessity
> written, it might be more accurate to say that language
> for pornography is a prison from which it is continually
> trying to escape. At best, language is a bothersome neces-
> sity, for its function in pornography is to set going a series
> of non-verbal images, of fantasies, and if it could achieve
> this without the mediation of words it would. (p. 282)

This may be true of *The Lustful Turk*, despite Marcus's own
special pleading for its literary excellences, but it is hardly
the case for *My Secret Life*, which Marcus consistently patron-
izes and denigrates. The best effects in *My Secret Life* are
clearly those of literature and not pornography.

Marcus's final argument is even more objectionable than
the other two: pornography, as opposed to literature, vio-
lates the psychological complexity of human beings and
their relations. Literature

> proceeds by elaboration, the principal means of this elab-
> oration being the imagination of situations of conflict
> between persons or within a single person. All of these
> interests are antagonistic to pornography. Pornography
> is not interested in persons but in organs. Emotions are
> an embarrassment to it, and motives are distractions. . . .
> Sex in pornography is sex without the emotions.(p.284)

To return to *My Secret Life*, which is the focus of Marcus's
study, why would anyone conceivably read it if the author
were simply 'not interested in persons but in organs'? Walter

is obviously interested in persons. He is trapped in his compulsive obsession with sex, and his autobiography is psychologically energized by this obsession.

Marcus scornfully dismisses the kind of pornography that is badly written and that no one would want to read. In fact a work need not be pornographic at all to fulfill all of Marcus's criteria. It seems to me that Marcus has used pornography as a convenient category in which to dump all the characteristics of bad fiction. But as Taylor Stoehr has so acutely discerned in 'Pornography, masturbation and the novel', the question must be engaged at a much deeper level of awareness, because 'the novel has defined itself historically in just the terms Marcus uses to condemn pornography' (p. 40). Ned Polsky also inveighs against *The Other Victorians* as 'a prime instance of rubbishy "sociologizing" about pornography, "sociologizing" of the sort produced by that growing band of literary critics who believe they are experts on society simply because they live in it' (p. 202).

The same argument applies to films. In the sleazy realm of X-rated movies, as soon as a film is disturbing and impinges on some emotional reality, like Paul Morrissey's *Trash*, it becomes art and not pornography. By the customary definition, dirty movies cannot be art; if they are art, they therefore cannot be dirty movies. Nagisa Oshima's *In the Realm of the Senses* is an extraordinary study of sexual obsession, both psychotic and romantic – it is a sexually explicit Japanese version of Bo Widerberg's *Elvira Madigan* – that can only end in castration, dismemberment and death. *In the Realm of the Senses* is an art film that depends completely on the materials and conventions of pornographic movies. To exclude it from pornography merely because it is so successful seems to me to beg the question. Oshima could not have begun to make his movie without a strong and clearly defined tradition of pornography on which he could draw.

The issue is amusingly debated in Terry Southern's wild and raunchy novel, *Blue Movie*, where the great director Boris Adrian, displeased with the stag movies he has just seen, poses some difficult questions about cinematic sex:

> He was aware that the freedom of expression and development in cinema had always lagged behind that of literature, as, until recent years, it had lagged behind that of the theater as well. Eroticism of the most aesthetic and creatively effective nature abounded in every form of contemporary prose – why had it not been achieved, or even seriously attempted, on film? Was there something inherently alien to eroticism in the medium of film? Something too personal to share with an audience? (p. 25)

The answer to these theoretical questions is the super-sex movie, *The Faces of Love*, that Boris makes on a three million dollar budget in Liechtenstein. It will be the first 'really *good*' pornographic movie, 'genuinely erotic and beautiful' (p. 29).

With this dubious background of equivocation and circular reasoning, 'pornography' is obviously a term to be avoided. Instead we will use the more neutral phrase 'sexual fiction' to define our subject. It is intentionally broad enough to include all narrative material that makes important and open use of sexual activity as its subject matter. In sexual fiction the interest in sexuality is continuous throughout the book and not just confined to certain episodes. Joyce's *Ulysses*, for example, is brilliantly sexual in Molly Bloom's final soliloquy and also in Leopold Bloom's sexual preoccupations during his day in Dublin, but it is not primarily a sexual novel. Incidentally, we know from some recently published letters that Joyce wrote to his wife that he was experimenting with the grossly masturbatory prose of 'dirty' books. Sexual fiction focusses on erotic themes, just as science fiction emphasizes science, technology and cosmology, detective novels depend on the solution of murders, and thrillers seek to involve us actively in a web of suspense. I believe that sexual fiction is a legitimate literary genre (or sub-genre), with its own set of assumptions and expectations. If it is dull, mindless, predictable and mechanical, it is unsuccessful both in its literary and in its sexual expression. There can only be one set of criteria for the excellent and the meretricious in sexual fiction as well as in any other kind of literature.

A great deal has been written on sexual themes in literature, especially along the lines of Ralph Ginzburg's leering and ignorant *An Unhurried View of Erotica*, but there is surprisingly little serious criticism of sexual fiction. Most notable in this area is Susan Sontag's *Partisan Review* essay, 'The pornographic imagination', which is included in *Styles of Radical Will* and reprinted in Douglas A. Hughes's excellent collection, *Perspectives on Pornography*. With quiet authority and using examples drawn mostly from contemporary French literature, Sontag insists that 'some pornographic books are interesting and important as works of art' (p. 183). She thus systematically demolishes Steven Marcus's judgment of pornography as outside the pale of literature.

Michael Perkins makes a similar defense of modern erotic literature in *The Secret Record*, which is especially devoted to the publications of Olympia Press and Essex House. For Perkins, sexual fiction can be justified on three grounds: assaultive, seductive and philosophical. 'The assaultive mode of erotic writing involves the extreme expression of the anarchic impulse in eroticism. Its aggressive, brutal images are designed to shock the reader into an awareness of the destructive, usually repressed aspect of his own erotic feelings' (p. 210). The seductive mode arouses a sympathetic sexual response and mirrors the reader's own erotic nature. In the philosophical mode, intellectual speculations about the nature of eroticism are explored, and especially the conscious and unconscious impulses by which we understand both the meaning of death and the transcendence of self through eroticism.

This book is chiefly concerned with the fiction-making, fantasizing impulse of sexual writing and its stylistic and thematic assumptions. At some point the line between fiction and non-fiction is hard to draw. Are the sexual fantasies in Nancy Friday's *My Secret Garden* wish-fulfillment or reality? Are they projections, exaggerations, compensations or just simply story-telling? There is no way to refer these letters (and interviews) back to any underlying reality. The same is true of the anonymous Victorian sexual autobiography, *My Secret Life*. Is it authentic? There is no way of knowing, so that we should rather ask: is it convincing? Does it convey a sense of verisimilitude? Does it impinge on identifiable realities, both sexual and psychological? In the absence of any external verification of 'Walter' and his secret life, we are forced to deal with his autobiography as a work of fiction. Sexual fiction obviously lends itself to the genre of true confessions. One of its most established conventions is for the author to take the reader into his confidence and to give him a glimpse into his Pandora's box of guilty and perhaps also debasing secrets. The illusion of confidence must pass muster for the illusion of reality, and the confessor bears strong resemblances to the literary type of the confidence man. In sexual fiction the reader stands in a naturally voyeuristic relation to the book, so that authors and readers alike are made to share a sense of complicity toward their subject.

The most striking feature of sexual fiction is its thorough sexualizing of reality. All perception is eroticized and the world becomes, as in Leo Bersani's formulation in *A Future for Astyanax*, a theater for the enactment of our desires, 'constantly open to – always ready to be penetrated by – our desires' (p. 308). In other words, what may be perceived as external reality is really a projection of our own sexual fantasies, as these have the power to transform the literal truth. One of the most powerful imaginative attractions of the Marquis de Sade is that he succeeds in creating a world apart – often a Gothic castle or abbey actually cut off from the world – in which old-fashioned religion and morality have been replaced by purely sexual mores and rules. This is 'sexual politics' in its most literal sense. Everything in this cruelly Hobbesian society is dominated by sex as the instrument of natural law and power. Nothing can be imagined apart from the tyrannous control of sex, which is the source of whatever order and stability remain in a world given up to the brute control of erotic impulse. This political view of Sade is the basis for Angela Carter's dazzling book, *The Sadeian Woman and the Ideology of Pornography*.

Sade's frenzied vision is much more fully realized than the mild, pastoral 'pornotopia' of Steven Marcus in *The Other Victorians*, which is a parody of beneficent utopian imaginings:

> All men in it are always and infinitely potent; all women fecundate with lust and flow inexhaustibly with sap or juice or both. Everyone is always ready for anything, and everyone is infinitely generous with his substance. It is always summertime in pornotopia, and it is a summertime of the emotions as well – no one is ever jealous, possessive, or really angry. All our aggressions are perfectly fused with our sexuality, and the only rage is the rage of lust, a happy fury indeed. (p. 276)

It is surprising that Marcus's pornotopia should so rigorously exclude any harshness or boredom or pain. For all of his infantile self-indulgence, Sade at least presents us with an erotic world that is frighteningly real in its psychological immediacy. It is the nightmare of infinite consummation, the literalizing of Blake's 'lineaments of gratified desire' ('The Question Answer'd').

In the introduction to what promises to be a massive series of volumes on the history of sexuality, Michel Foucault is very preoccupied with the interest in 'transforming sex into discourse' (p. 20) that began in the seventeenth century and can be seen so vividly in a new form of detailed sexual inquiry that established itself through the Catholic confessional. One implication of Foucault's thesis is that in the seventeenth century sex is also being transformed into the stuff of fiction; it is being shaped and made available as a literary subject. In other words, a habit of sexual introspection provides us with a way of interpreting character and motive that feeds the early development of the novel. As a formalization of human experience, the novel depends very heavily on sexual manifestations, no matter how covertly hidden by the author's proprieties. Thus Richardson's *Pamela* (1740–1), in its primness and hot inhibitions, triggered a more overt and healthy sexuality in Fielding's *Shamela* (1741) and *Joseph Andrews* (1742) and also quite possibly in Cleland's consciously erotic *Fanny Hill* (1749). Pamela is a little volcano of sexuality, as the titillating pressures build up over hundreds and hundreds of pages toward her giant eruption. The genius of the novel form, as Foucault indicates, seems to lie in its enormous productivity of sexual discourse, which is inherently more exciting than sexual activity. Sexual discourse is a self-conscious and self-regarding system, a channel of endless introspection, psychological analysis and moral evaluation.

Foucault owes an obvious debt to Roland Barthes's studies of Sade, which first appeared in book form in 1971 (translated into English as *Sade Fourier Loyola* in 1976). What is so remarkable about these brilliant essays is Barthes's insistence that eroticism is a highly formalized mode of ordering experience, essentially a mode of discourse:

> For Sade, there is no eroticism unless the crime is 'reasoned'; to *reason* means to philosophize, to dissertate, to harangue, in short, to subject crime (a generic term designating all the Sadeian passions) to a system of articulated language; but it also means to combine according to precise rules the specific actions of vice, so as to make from these series and groups of actions a new 'language', no longer spoken but acted; a 'language' of crime, or new code of love, as elaborate as the code of courtly love. (p. 27)

Barthes quotes the telling line from Sade's *Juliette*, 'we soon lit the flame of passion from the torch of philosophy', and he notes with characteristic insight that Sade 'makes sperm the substitute for speech (and not the opposite), describing it in the same terms applied to the orator's art' (p. 32). In short, for Sade the erotic is a form of imaginative rhetoric with its own strict rules and conventions. The role of libertine and victim is defined by the use of a certain kind of language. They are 'language actors' (Barthes, p. 145) rather than flesh-and-blood characters in a narrative that has only the most tenuous relation to the physiology of sexual experience in the real world.

William Gass takes these theories as far as they will go in his 'philosophical inquiry', *On Being Blue*, in which sexual activity can only be rationalized as providing the raw materials of sexual discourse:

> the ultimate and essential displacement is to the word
> . . . . the true sexuality in literature – sex as a positive aesthetic quality – lies not in any scene and subject, nor in the mere appearance of a vulgar word, not in the thick smear of a blue spot, but in the consequences on the page of love well made – made to the medium which is the writer's own . . . what counts is not what lascivious sights your loins can tie to your thoughts like Lucky is to Pozzo, but love lavished on speech of any kind, regardless of content and intention. (p. 43)

This is disturbingly solipsistic and seems to require that raw experience must be aesthetically perfected in the mind of the perceiver. Thus sexuality, in Gass's view, only exists as a projection of language back into physical events: 'not the language of love, but the love of language, not matter, but meaning, not what the tongue touches, but what it forms, not lips and nipples, but nouns and verbs' (p. 11). By its abstraction *On Being Blue* becomes an anti-erotic book. It doesn't sexualize reality; rather it intellectualizes sexuality. In Foucault, Barthes and Gass we must accept the radical notion that sexuality only exists as a form of discourse, that without language sexuality as such would cease to be. Nabokov's *Lolita* offers one answer to this dualistic dilemma, because it manages to bridge the gap between artful discourse and heavy-breathing sensuality.

To look at the other side of the question, does sexual fiction need to arouse us physically – to 'turn us on' – in order to be effective? We know that Masters and Johnson used erotica to stimulate their laboratory subjects, or at least the electrodes implanted in their subjects, but we also know that they used a vibrator to produce at least fifty multiple orgasms. What does that prove? Does tragedy need to make us cry or comedy make us laugh in order to be successful? We often laugh or weep for extraneous and unworthy reasons. Laughter and tears cannot by themselves be the criteria for comedy and tragedy, just as orgasm cannot possibly be the touchstone for sexual fiction. It is writing not life that we are dealing with, so that if we are moved, there must be some vision of life intensely depicted by which we judge the quality of the work. We must be made to feel the meaningfulness of the deaths in tragedy, the marriages in comedy and the orgasms (or lack of orgasms) in sexual fiction.

Although orgasm is a species of fulfillment that allies sexual fiction with comedy, I believe that sexual fiction stimulates feelings and excellences of its own that are different from either comedy or tragedy. The most important of these differences is the powerful evocation of a sexual, eroticized reality. This can create a unique sense of moral or amoral possibility in which the characters try to work out their destiny in relation to the irrational pull of desire. In sexual fiction there is an intense concentration on a few physical combinations, so that repetition can hypnotically narrow our focus on crucial psychological truths. The artistry lies in the versatile and profound use of extremely limited resources. Merely to understand the imperious force of sexual impulses is itself an induction into the reality of human psychology. Although sexual fiction has its own characteristic qualities, these are allied in a continuum with the excellences of other fiction. There are no special evaluative procedures for sexual fiction; it has to be judged by the same criteria as all other literature.

The chapters that follow move in a propositional and comparative direction. The intent of this book is to explore a relatively uncharted subject in order to discover its typical assumptions and conventions. We will be specially concerned with the stylistic expression of many repeated images and patterns of discourse. Certain crucial questions arise from the consideration of sexual fiction as a genre. The first chapter therefore serves as an overture, since it explores some of the preoccupations of the genre. Sexual fantasy and wish-fulfillment generate a characteristic repertory of themes. We draw on the women's fantasies collected by Nancy Friday in *My Secret Garden*. These represent an anthology of sexual fabulation, which is surprisingly resistant to the new sexual physiology (as in Mary Jane Sherfey's *The Nature and Evolution of Female Sexuality*) and the new sexual sociology (most notably Shere Hite's *The Hite Report*). It is paradoxical that sexual biology plays so minor a role in sexual fantasizing. It is almost as if the two were antagonistic systems.

The literary sequence is not precisely chronological, although there is a general movement from the older literature to the more modern. We begin with the Marquis de Sade not because sadomasochism is central to our concerns, but because Sade so overwhelmingly dominates and permeates any consideration of sexual writing. There is nothing of importance in this subject that does not appear somewhere in his voluminous pages. He is an intensely pessimistic, naturalistic philosopher, who sexualizes all of reality. Sade set out not only to outrage human decencies, but also to force us to answer him. We follow this existentialist line in Chapter 3 with *Story of O* by Pauline Réage and *The Image* by Jean de Berg, both books directly in the tradition of Sade. In their sadomasochistic theatricalization of sex, *Story of O* and *The Image* tease us with philosophical paradoxes: ecstasy or degradation, self-annihilation or self-exaltation, religion or blasphemy? Their cruel sexuality is endowed with the martyrdom of religious experience, and the torments are heightened by aesthetic detail. With great ceremoniousness, they insist on costume, make-up, perfume, the look and feel of textures – all perhaps related to the art of photography and the photographer's models who figure in these pages.

Chapter 4 sets out to compare the representation of sexuality in two classics of English sexual fiction: the eighteenth-century *Memoirs of a Woman of Pleasure* (popularly called *Fanny Hill*) and the Victorian sexual autobiography, *My Secret Life*. Unlike Sade and his followers, Cleland depicts a joyous, pastoral sexuality in *Fanny Hill*, which replaces any earthy, four-letter words with a euphemistic, hyperbolic and highly metaphorized vocabulary. Sex is not only poetic in *Fanny Hill*, it also leads to good fortune and success in life. Both Fanny and Walter (the anonymous author of *My Secret Life*) are sexual entrepreneurs, since both devote their lives exclusively to sex. There is, however, a certain grimness in the compulsive sexuality of *My Secret Life*. It is frank, intense, repetitive and physiological in a way calculated to shock any purely hedonistic expectations.

The central question of sexuality and values – the life force, lifestyle, the good life, self-fulfillment – lies behind Chapters 5 and 6, in which D. H. Lawrence's *Lady Chatterley's Lover* is set against Henry Miller's *Tropic of Cancer*, and Philip Roth's *Portnoy's Complaint* is paired with Erica Jong's *Fear of Flying*. Lawrence is the strongest proselytizer for sex in this group. His romantic emphasis on the instinctual life, the urges of the body over the desiccated theorizing of the mind, leads naturally to an exaltation of the phallic mysteries of sex. Connie rediscovers her blood lust and is thereby reborn to a new life: sex has the quality of religious illumination. Miller also celebrates sex, but in a less programmatic and more Whitmanesque style. Sex is part of everything that flows: food, drink, street life, conversation, poetry. Roth and Jong represent a more contemporary and more neurotic use of sexual themes. They are both steeped in guilt, frustration and self-sacrifice that seem specifically Jewish in the sense of Gerald Rosen's mock quotation from Confucius: 'When you're in love, the whole world is Jewish' (epigraph to *The Carmen Miranda Memorial Flagpole*, 1979). Sex represents the unattainable life of pleasure, the id, ecstatic and irresponsible happiness. Roth is wonderfully compassionate to adolescent blockages, and Jong tries hard to delineate a distinctively feminine consciousness. Both authors, and especially Roth, use satire and a frenzied humor to grapple with a resistant sexual identity. In classic Freudian style, the laughter is a way of mastering sexual anxieties.

The final chapter explores some of the sexual values of a consumerist culture as expressed in Gael Greene's *Blue Skies, No Candy*, Terry Southern and Mason Hoffenberg's *Candy*, and Vladimir Nabokov's *Lolita*. All three novels are highly parodic, mocking the conspicuous consumption and the status consciousness of the societies they depict. Sex is performative, with its own implied warranty of function according to specifications. The characters have been programmed to conform to the emotional needs of high technology. They are thus both romantic and mechanistic, and sex is not a natural force at all, but a product of art and the marketplace. Sex is an aesthetic, solid-state, disposable commodity of a pleasure-loving society. It is the ultimate Madison Avenue hype, so that we are made acutely aware of having the kind and variety of sex appropriate to our economic position. There is an upward mobility in sexual experience that reflects our status in the social hierarchy – we tune in to our proper frequency. Thus sexual literature can serve as a satiric vehicle for cultural mythology, expressing it, confirming it and making fun of it at the same time.

1 PHYSIOLOGY AND FANTASY:
the facts of life and *My Secret Garden*

A TEASING paradox of sexual literature is the lack of relation between biology and the imagination, between the facts of life and the processing of these facts in sexual fiction, between our ever-increasing knowledge of sexual physiology and the wild and unrestrained operations of sexual fantasy. In literature, at least, biology is not destiny, and the depiction of sexuality, especially female sexuality, has been very little influenced by new biological and socio-sexual findings. It is as if the fantasy themes that emerge in literature arise from needs and wish-fulfillments that are impervious to physical fact. This separateness of sexual fiction confirms its mental, ideational, ritualistic and imaginative character. In some important ways the literature defies the physiological reality of sexual experience, but it is also possible that sexual experience itself is shaped by fictional rather than physiological scenarios.

Even the most explicitly physical sex manual is interpreted in the mode of pornography rather than practical instruction, and bookstores never classify the 'how to' sex books with other self-improvement materials on tennis, golf, swimming, etc. It is assumed that, except in movies like Gene Wilder's *The World's Greatest Lover*, these sex manuals will not be used for actual, on-the-job training. The frank, educational pictures in these books feature attractive, professional models who follow the conventional postures and gestures of dirty movies, which probably owe a great deal to the tradition of sexual illustration in books such as Aretino's *Postures* (*c*. 1524). David Foxon's study of libertine literature confirms the highly traditional character of sexual iconography. Alex Comfort's enormously popular *Joy of Sex* (and its joyous spinoffs on gay sex and lesbian sex) use very soft, sensuous and fuzzily romantic drawings. The bearded male hero is not at all like the macho plumber type played by Harry Reems in many X-rated movies, but a sophisticated fantasy figure who can serve as a model for upper-middle-class, middle-aged lust; he is the gigolo type, updated and upgraded. And the woman is thin, svelte, not over-developed, educated and rather plain-looking – the kind of woman one might meet in Bloomingdale's or Harrod's. The illustrators have gone out of their way not to offend against good taste – these are not the boy and girl next door or any identifiable persons, but idealized figures of sexual fantasy like a remote and wealthy aunt and uncle about whom we have great expectations.

It is alarming to discover in *The Hite Report* that 'only approximately 30 percent of the women in this study could orgasm regularly from intercourse' (p. 136), a statistic generally confirmed in Seymour Fisher's massive study, *The Female Orgasm* (and in the briefer summary of findings, *Understanding the Female Orgasm*), and supported by Mary Jane Sherfey's *The Nature and Evolution of Female Sexuality* as well as by Kinsey's *Sexual Behavior in the Human Female* and Masters and Johnson's *Human Sexual Response*. All of this formidable literature stresses the inadequacy of clitoral stimulation during sexual union. It could be understood as a covert attack – overt in *The Hite Report* – on vaginal intercourse as a model for heterosexuality, since the clitoris is so well designed as a sexual organ, while the vagina is poorly supplied with the proper nerve endings. The perversity of nature in having switched around, as it were, the human female's sexual equipment would have delighted the Marquis de Sade, who scorned and loathed the 'seat of nature' in woman and enjoyed seeing natural law subverted.

Thus, from a neurological point of view, male penetration is not the optimum way for a woman to receive sexual pleasure. Just the contrary. Penetration should be delayed for as long as possible, and foreplay maximally extended so that the clitoris may be adequately stimulated. In the meantime the deep, fully genital, adult and mature vaginal orgasm of the Freudians has been exploded as a biological myth, while the clitoral orgasm, much scorned by the Freudians and D. H. Lawrence for its immature, neurotic and masturbatory character, is now understood to be the only true orgasm experienced by a woman. Perhaps the more intense clitoral orgasm is the equivalent of what was once thought to be the vaginal orgasm. In any case the vaginal orgasm has more or less disappeared from serious consideration as a separate sexual experience.

Mary Jane Sherfey's physiological (and especially embryological) treatise, *The Nature and Evolution of Female Sexuality*, is designed to demonstrate women's sexual superiority to men She claims as a well-known fact that women have much greater sexual capacity than men. One of the most far-reaching hypotheses extrapolated from Sherfey's data is the

> universal and physically normal condition of women's inability ever to reach complete sexual satiation in the presence of the most intense, repetitive orgasmic experiences, no matter how produced. Theoretically, a woman could go on having orgasms indefinitely if physical exhaustion did not intervene. (pp. 134–5)

There is, of course, a distinction between sexual satisfaction and sexual satiation. Although Masters say that 'a woman *will usually* be satisfied with 3–5 orgasms', Sherfey believes that

> it would rarely be said, 'a man will usually be satisfied with three to five ejaculations'. The man *is* satisfied. The woman *usually wills* herself to be satisfied because she is simply unaware of the extent of her orgasmic capacity. (p. 135)

Since most sexual books are written by men, they rarely project woman's tremendous orgasmic capacity, except as an expression of nymphomania, and in literature nymphomania is understood, incorrectly, as a tribute to the man's power to arouse a woman almost to the point of madness – an unquenchable fire that repeated sexual experiences only intensify.

Sherfey is quick to draw the obvious social implications of women's almost unlimited sexual powers:

> Women's inordinate orgasmic capacity did not evolve for monogamous, sedentary cultures. It is unreasonable to expect that this inordinate sexual capacity could be, even in part, given expression within the confines of our culture . . . . Neither men nor women, but especially not women, are biologically built for the single spouse, monogamous marital structure or for the prolonged adolescence which our society can now bestow upon both of them. (p. 137)

Sherfey goes so far as to postulate a period in prehistory when women's inordinate sexual demands had to be forcefully suppressed in order to establish modern civilization as we know it: 'Primitive woman's sexual drive was too strong, too susceptible to the fluctuating extremes of an impelling, aggressive eroticism to withstand the disciplined requirements of a settled family life' (p. 138). For literature, these speculations would generate an Amazonian fiction along the lines of Monique Wittig's *Les Guérillères*. Sherfey's biological portrait of women is certainly different from the passive/submissive creatures of sexual fiction who need men to complete their being. Sherfey's model woman has tremendous sexual vitality; she is hardly a hole (void, gap, slit, lacuna) waiting to be filled (and thereby brought to life) by the male penis.

We could go on presenting the findings of the new sexual physiology. These socio-medical studies make up a small library of spicy scientific works that have had a much wider readership than was ever imagined by their publishers –

more than half of Shere Hite's monumental survey, for example, is devoted to masturbation, orgasm, intercourse and clitoral stimulation, and she prints extracts from her respondents' questionnaires that are frankly erotic. It is curious but predictable that the male answer to *The Hite Report*, Anthony Pietropinto and Jacqueline Simenauer's *Beyond the Male Myth*, is so mild and so profoundly lacking in seriousness. Men tended to give flippant, defensive answers and to rate sex below work and personal achievement. Thus one respondent gave the following priorities: '(1) Striving for successful business career (2) Consumption of food and beverage (3) Need for seven hours of sleep per night (4) Participation in sex, regularly' (p. 81). Another ranked sex 'a close second behind flying as a job. I can spend a hell of a lot more time flying than I can screwing' (p. 81). A third judged sex to be 'cool', but 'Drag racing is more to my attitude' (p. 81).

Beyond the Male Myth is a good example of the intense polarization of male and female attitudes. Even if we disagree with the authors' sampling and interviewing techniques – and especially with their use of a professional market-survey company to do the basic work – we must still account for the fact that men and women, at least in America, have a radically different orientation to sex. In *The Hite Report* sex is a crisis subject that evokes a strong sense of aggression against men for dominating women and ignoring their needs. In *Beyond the Male Myth* sex is a form of recreation set apart from the ordinary concerns of life; women are valued insofar as they satisfy male needs and enact male scenarios. In other words speculations about men tend to dominate *The Hite Report*, whereas women do not dominate *Beyond the Male Myth*. They are seen as projections of male desires and fantasies and therefore remain shadowy and peripheral throughout this long book. These disappointing conclusions about male sexual fantasy are abundantly confirmed by Nancy Friday's new collection, *Men in Love* (1980), whose male correspondents are shockingly prosaic, unimaginative and trivial.

The male–female polarity has important consequences for a study of sexual fiction. Most of the books are written by men, and even those written by women, such as Erica Jong's *Fear of Flying* and Gael Greene's *Blue Skies, No Candy*, are not definitively feminine (although Jong is certainly more so than Greene). It is still an open question whether there could be an entirely different sexual fiction written by women. One could argue that the sexual books by women express more tender feelings and are more oriented to emotions aroused by sexuality. Their erotic sensibility is more global and not necessarily localized in the erogenous zones. This is true even of the highly colored, very poeti- cized erotica written by Anaïs Nin and recently published in *Delta of Venus* and *Little Birds*. But she uses male models for her primary action and structure, so that the erotic vignettes exist to satisfy male lust and were, in fact, paid for by the page by a rich collector of curiosa. In *Fear of Flying* Isadora menstruates at the end of the novel, an activity generally taboo in sexual fiction, but even in the act of repossessing her own body in the steamy bath, she still needs a man to complete and fulfill her being.

Paradoxically, although sexual fiction is written primarily by men and according to male values, its subject is almost entirely female sexuality. It is as if this is a central, compel- ling mystery, which no one can ever hope to understand. Feminine psychology is endlessly explored, especially erotic psychology, but no firm conclusions are drawn. Male sexuality remains sketchy and shadowy – a powerful and irresist- ible force in the background. Thus Mellors the game- keeper in Lawrence's *Lady Chatterley's Lover* is vague and unrealized as a character. He is an idealized male presence (or Lawrence's idea of maleness), but Connie's sexual awakening lies at the heart of the book. Similarly in *Story of O* both René and Sir Stephen and the other men at Roissy and elsewhere (including the Commander at the end) are uncharacterized male figures, radiating a cruel sexuality it is true, but not expressing the intense fictional life of O, who thinks, reasons and feels, and is not merely a sexual symbol.

Why are the men such blank ciphers in this book? Their hovering emptiness indicates that they have already undergone some powerful dehumanization before O goes to Roissy. Will the new feminine sexual literature focus on men and on male sexuality? I suspect not, because the sexual books by women we already have are preoccupied with their own modified version of female sexuality.

To return to the physiological and psycho-sexual questions with which this chapter began, it should be obvious that biology cannot provide us with a baseline or touchstone or criterion for sexual fiction. Just the opposite seems to be true, and sexual fiction proceeds without any significant reference to biological truth. Its women are always well lubricated and fully orgasmic, elaborate foreplay is rendered unnecessary by the sheer intensity of passionate attraction, and male penetration provides the ultimate climax of ecstatic sexual union. Despite that small minority of women in *The Hite Report* regularly experiencing orgasm during vaginal intercourse, these are nevertheless the wish-fulfillment fantasies of a male-oriented literature. Yet they have the magical power to establish the assumptions and conventions of sexual fiction. In *My Secret Life*, although Walter has had sex with 'something like twelve hundred women . . . of twenty-seven different empires, kingdoms or countries, and eighty or more different nationalities, including every one in Europe except a Laplander' (p. 618), not a one has ever failed to drench herself with anticipatory, pre-coital pleasure and to have a series of ever more powerful and more devastating orgasms. Walter's statistics do not fit well with those of Shere Hite and others, so that we are evidently in the presence of two irreconcilable systems, both equally 'true' in their own perceptual world.

The women's fantasies collected by Nancy Friday in *My Secret Garden* (and in a weak sequel, *Forbidden Flowers*) offer representative samples of the feminine imagination (male fantasies appear in *Men in Love*). They are the 'real' fantasies of presumably real women who answered the author's ads in various publications and some of whom participated in taped interviews, although there is always the lingering suspicion that, like the proverbial Miss Lonelyhearts column, much of the material may have been written by the fiendishly clever author. *My Secret Garden* is useful for our purposes because it provides us with the raw materials of sexual fiction, a repertory of sexual themes and preoccupations that were voluntarily recorded by a large group of fantasizing women. The writing seems to be influenced by sexual fiction, especially of the romantic, power-oriented, ego-enhancing, melodramatic sort. It is 'pre-fictional', if we may coin a term for plotting and characterization that hover between the naked wish-fulfillment of dreams – the kind of unselfconscious narrative one finds in letters and transcripts of conversations – and unconscious imitations of magazine fiction and the situational soap operas of television. The best fantasies suggest an ambiguous relation to real life, and some actually cross over into the happy ending of realization. The writing then becomes a form of retrospective, self-fulfilling prophecy on how to make your sexual fantasies come true. The fantasy format allows for unrestrained erotic writing under the non-fiction, true-story formula, and the author is full of self-righteousness about her self-help mission.

From the perspective of *My Secret Garden*, the sociosexual, physiological literature we have been discussing does not exist. There is no awareness in this book of up-to-date biological thinking on sexual matters, nor is there anything but the dimmest consciousness of women's liberation themes as they might apply to sexual politics. This seems especially surprising in a book put together from the contributions of about 400 women. Sexuality is understood almost entirely as a pyschological rather than a physical activity. It is related to ego needs and satisfactions rather than bodily needs, and it is not surprising that the fantasies are so overwhelming narcissistic. In other words the fantasies project a desirable, attractive, romantic and powerful image of the self that is presumably absent from real life. The scenarios imagined are adventurous and compensatory; they fulfill longings for power, importance, luxury and the hypnotic control over others through sexual charisma.

One dominant theme is exhibitionism. The women imagine themselves in spectacular situations where they are admired and desired by multitudes of enthralled men. Celeste's fantasy is naively typical:

> I'm on one of those stirrup tables that gynecologists have, where they spread your legs and look deep into you. But the table is in the middle of the ring, in Madison Square Garden, and it's mounted on a revolving platform. Thousands of men have paid fifty or a hundred dollars each for tickets, and the ushers are selling binoculars so they can get a better view. I tell Charlie that the table is slowly turning around and around, with the bright lights illuminating me, and the men in the seats all around begin pushing forward, jumping out of their seats, the whole giant mob wild with excitement to see, thousands and thousands of men in a circle all around me, all wild with excitement to see me better, to fuck me, to get deep inside those wet, red lips they can see so plainly. (p. 107)

This is at once reassuring and ominous, because Celeste needs the mob scene of a boxing or wrestling match in order to excite herself, but she is also proud of her extraordinary fascination and control. It is, after all, just a performance, and she knows that her faithful and modest Charlie 'is waiting for me in a dressing room off-stage where he has a warm bed . . .'. It looks as if the whole fantasy is designed to excite Charlie to new heights of sexual performance.

Celeste's theatricalization of her sexuality is almost literally transposed in the fantasy of Caroline, the English actress, who is in a current West End play that requires her to be nude and to have sexual intercourse on stage. This is real life, but Caroline's secret imaginings show how fully she becomes immersed in her exhibitionistic role:

> As I got more and more used to the role, more comfortable in it, I found that instead of dreading the moment

when I had to begin, I was looking forward to it. My nipples would become tight and erect. It was a surprisingly seductive feeling, one I enjoyed. I began wearing tighter and tighter blouses, filmier ones, more see-through, so that the audience could see my excitement, could see the excitement I felt right down – or up – to my nipples. I needed the audience's excitement for my own ... a form of complicity was set up between them and me, a sexual conspiracy which heightened my ability, or rather, desire to play the part. (p. 103)

In the end, Caroline comes to need the audience to validate her sexual being, and making love in private becomes disappointing and anxiety provoking:

So even if I'm with the man I'm in love with, somehow in my mind I twist his face around so that it's the face of the actor I'm in the play with. The funny thing is, I don't even *like* the actor. Maybe that makes it even more exciting for me, I don't know. I haven't really figured this out. But I think it's because behind him, behind his back is the audience, and they're applauding him for making love to me and applauding me for responding to him in such a loving way. (p. 104)

Caroline desperately needs the approbation of an audience in order to function sexually. Her private life seems to have disappeared, so that without the audience she is a sexual nonentity. She has fictionalized her private life in order to sexualize it, and one has the impression that her sexual theatricalizing is necessary to overcome frigidity.

The serpent hidden in *My Secret Garden* is rape, and the rape fantasy pervades almost all the confessions in direct or indirect form. But it is rape with a difference. The fantasy rape is a privileged and protected situation in which the creator can experience simultaneously the vicarious adventures of the fiction and also the mastery of its dangers. The rape fantasy offers a way of controlling fears about rape. The rapist is a dark and mysterious stranger, powerful and physically attractive, who is uncontrollably aroused by the beautiful woman. She submits to incontrovertible force, but the rapist is also sensitive to the woman's needs, and he is also imagined to be under her spell. By these romantic contradictions, the involuntary sexual experience becomes deeply moving and harm is averted.

In Julietta's fantasy the rape scenario is extended by having a male protector who gives the woman to a group of men:

> I imagine that I've been brought to some warehouse, or place like that, against my will. I'm stripped naked and the only thing I'm allowed to wear is a black silk mask. This is because whatever powerful person has brought me there does not want the men – yes, always more than one in this fantasy – for whom he has procured me, to know who I am. In this way, though he's brought me there against my will, he somehow wants to protect me too. I never know who he is, and he himself never fucks me. I just know that he's somewhere in the background, enjoying this feeling of power he has, not only over me, but over the men, too. That's because they're so hot with desire for me that they can barely control themselves. But he can take me away from them whenever he wants to. (pp. 110–11)

Julietta is very proud of her power to arouse a whole group of powerfully built men, but although she reiterates that it is all 'against her will', it is according to her own fantasy that she disposes of her body. Her own interpretation of her narrative provides the guilty key: she is in active rebellion against her mother's 'good little Julie', yet she still wants to preserve her innocence by fantasizing that 'I'm doing it against my will. That I'm being forced by the man's overwhelming physical strength.' In this way her guilt is both aroused and assuaged and the rape fantasy becomes titillating.

The fantasy of sex with an anonymous stranger is part of the rape fantasy. Here too a dangerous situation is not only controlled but also made gratifying to the perceiver. The male is unimportant and doesn't need either to be named, identified or characterized: he is a sex object. As in Mary Jane Sherfey's vision of ancient matriarchies, a group of powerful and sexually insatiable women use up a whole army of drone-like, anonymous males in endless intercourse. They are not named because they are not important enough or dignified enough to have any identity; they have only a sexual function. In *My Secret Garden*, Suzanne's fantasy is a simple, folktale narrative:

> she was alone in the cloakroom at a dance, bending forward, when a man came in behind her, lifted her dress, put his penis into her (obviously before the days of tights) and had intercourse with her without her looking around or even knowing who the man was. (p. 25)

This is not technically rape, since the element of force is missing, but an irresistible power renders the girl completely passive. The psychological factors are simplified, as in dreams, so that the girl never turns around or finds out who the man is. Actually her natural curiosity is so numbed that she never desires to see him. It is important to Suzanne that, as in *Story of O*, she be 'always available': 'The idea of the anonymous approach from behind continues to excite me ... the man would always do whatever he wanted without any form of lead up or courting' (p. 26). Any foreplay is effectively ruled out, so that the act of intercourse becomes a magical and instantaneous union. Elsewhere this archetypal male figure is called an 'impersonal manipulator' (p. 316). It is necessary for the fantasy that he not be identified in any way – that he remain completely depersonalized.

In Pamela's fantasy, the deserted beach scene is the dreamlike setting for a narrative of desire in which the end is already implicit in the beginning. Although Pamela says that she is lying on her back 'sound asleep', she is nevertheless fully aware of what is happening:

> I am wearing only a bikini, the bottom part fastened on each side with only a tiny bow, and the top fastened in

front only with a bow, too, between my enormous breasts, which are already almost overwhelming the little bit of cloth that is the bra. I breathe deeply and evenly, shifting positions lightly as I sleep. A man's shadow falls across me; he stands looking down at me as I sleep. He's very tanned and wears only swimming trunks. He watches, and as he watches me sleeping he gets excited. He kneels beside me, very softly and gently so as not to awaken me, and very carefully unties the bow at one of my hips, then reaches over me to untie the other side. He lays the bikini back, exposing me to his gaze. (p. 97)

Pamela's 'enormous' and 'overwhelming' breasts are an indication of her state of mind, which seems miraculously to produce the 'man's shadow' that falls across her. This is no ordinary rapist, but an incredibly tender and sensitive lover. The fantasy is strongly anchored in the voyeuristic myth of the man transfixed by the woman's dazzling beauty, who loses all responsibility for what he does. Although Pamela never opens her eyes, she does help to glide the stranger's penis into her and thereby begin the long-anticipated climax. The fantasy concludes by insisting on the separateness of the dreamer from the events that occur: 'But I never open my eyes, just murmur as if I were sleeping and enjoying a good dream' (p. 97). There is an important symbolic space between being 'sound asleep' at the start and 'as if I were sleeping' at the end, which acknowledges the sexual make-believe.

Readers will undoubtedly be reminded of Erica Jong's 'zipless fuck', a central concept in *Fear of Flying*. The zipless fuck is sex without stress, without anticipation, guilt or remorse, it is the ideal and pure love-making between absolute strangers. It is deliberately drained of love and responsibility – a spontaneous, highly idealized animal act that has special appeal to Hamlet-like intellectuals 'sicklied o'er with the pale cast of thought'. Erica Jong describes it in the ecstatic terms of fantasy:

The zipless fuck was more than a fuck. It was a platonic

ideal. Zipless because when you came together zippers fell away like rose petals, underwear blew off in one breath like dandelion fluff. Tongues intertwined and turned liquid. Your whole soul flowed out through your tongue and into the mouth of your lover. (p. 11)

Anonymity and brevity are essential to the zipless fuck

because the incident has all the swift compression of a dream and is seemingly free of all remorse and guilt; because there is no talk of her late husband or of his fiancée; because there is no rationalizing; because there is no talk at *all*. The zipless fuck is absolutely pure. It is free of ulterior motives. There is no power game. The man is not 'taking' and the woman is not 'giving'. No one is attempting to cuckold a husband or humiliate a wife. No one is trying to prove anything or get anything out of anyone. The zipless fuck is the purest thing there is. And it is rarer than the unicorn. And I have never had one. (p. 14)

In other words, it is sex completely dehumanized, desocial-ized and depersonalized, enacted effortlessly and magically through pure desire. All impediments disappear, both mat-erial (zippers, underwear) and physical (foreplay, clitoral stimulation, pre-coital lubrication, striving for mutual orgasm, etc.). The man and the woman are spiritually united in body, and, as in mystical trances, the sexual act is performed without any consciousness of time, mortality or worldly circumstance. There is no social or moral context. This is an archetypal sexual fantasy that is unrealizable by definition – in Erica Jong's apt phrase, a 'platonic ideal'.

A fourth theme of fantasy is the enormous penis that will fill every nook and cranny of female emptiness. This is clearly a folklore motif with no conceivable relation to sex-ual biology, and especially without any relevance to clitoral orgasm. Some of the fantasies about blacks depend on the myth of the enormous penis size of black men, a politically charged idea that Calvin C. Hernton explores in *Sex and Racism in America*. The desire and need to be filled would seem to be, on the surface, an expression of emptiness, but it may also be part of a sexual theme of abundance, plethora, excess, a cornucopia of satisfaction. To be filled is a step toward being overfilled, as flowing precedes overflowing. The penis is a fecundating force, which swells to bursting with its promise of pleasure and fertility. In Annabel's rape fantasy in *My Secret Garden* there is a progressive enlarging of the penis:

> I am being raped by not one man, but three or four. But the strange thing is that as each man takes his turn, I have to take a bigger penis. Some of the sizes of them in my fantasies are nine and twelve inches. And as I have to open my legs wide to take them, the erotic pleasure I have always brings on the most wonderful orgasm. (p. 58)

Sexual grandiosity is especially evident in animal fantasies, the wildest of which is that of Wanda and the donkey, which is also a rape fantasy. Wanda finds herself abducted to become the 'slave girl' of a party, where she is forced to have intercourse with a donkey. This is described in elaborate, sadomasochistic detail, but Wanda thinks of herself as not only experiencing a strange and unbelievable pleasure, but also acting in a heroic way to endure so much pain for the sake of such extraordinary ecstasy. The quantitative measure is literally a test of endurance and a proof of largeness of spirit; there is an exact ratio between the intensity of the trial and the magnitude of the triumph. These fantasies of penis size are everywhere evident in the writings of the Marquis de Sade.

A final theme in *My Secret Garden* is the grotesque sexualizing of daily life. Nancy Friday's respondents eroticize the routine chores of cleaning the house and cooking, and they manage to give a certain mock-heroic and bathetic quality to their inflamed imaginings. Esther's fantasy, for example, is at once comic, pathetic and touching, because her sexual scenario is played out in such a limited sphere:

> I do my housework in the tops of baby-doll pajamas, stay in a half-hot mood most of the time, what with touching

myself, or rubbing against different objects. The nozzle of the vacuum cleaner hose, for instance, played lightly over the pubic area is terrific and will bring on an orgasm if desired. Sometimes I wear a dildo inserted while doing housework. I imagine it to be my boxer dog's prick. (p. 67)

Like Garp's novel, *The World According to Bensenhaver* (interpolated into John Irving's *The World According to Garp*), this is sexual soap opera and also the conventional beginning of many X-rated movies, where a troubled housewife, scantily clad, anxiously awaits the arrival of the plumber. Esther gains verisimilitude by having a fantasy in which the parts of the vacuum cleaner play such an important role. Who can fail to identify with Esther as she prepares to confront another day in which she will be a psychically (but not a sexually) unemployed housewife?

Jo's fantasy is much more fully elaborated as a narrative, but it too begins with a classic erotic pattern for housewives:

I am alone in the house. My husband has left for work. I begin my housework downstairs, clearing the dishes from the dining room into the kitchen. I take off my nightgown and housecoat and work in the nude. (p. 166)

Clearly Jo has never bothered to dress for the day as she prepares for her secret life as sex-starved homemaker. The neighbor's dog, who follows her around, figures importantly in this fantasy. Jo busily seduces him in the kitchen with snacks of well-advertised products – Brand X is excluded, almost by definition, from sexual fiction. It is a food/sex fantasy of alarming dimensions, and the Betty Crocker chocolate cake (her husband's favorite dessert) baking in the oven represents the inevitable movement to orgasm:

The cake is getting larger and larger in the oven, so that it seems about to fill the oven, to push open the door and explode into the room, engulfing us in its sweet warmth. I pray that the dog will not stop and that the cake will not explode all over my nice clean kitchen before my husband gets home, before I am ready, before I have finished, before the dog has finished. (pp. 167–8)

Jo is as endearing a figure as Mrs Portnoy, with whom she shares the same anxieties about her 'nice clean kitchen'. With stunning contradiction she is both Mom with her Betty Crocker chocolate cake in the oven and a crazed nymphomaniac having strenuous intercourse with her neighbor's dog. Throughout *My Secret Garden* we are made to feel the intense loneliness of housewives all over America who, in the absence of affectionate human beings, are fantasizing (or actually having) intercourse with friendly dogs. This is a sexual preoccupation of Nancy Friday's book, and it conveys, from avowedly non-fictional sources, a grotesque image of America not unlike that of Nabokov's *Lolita*. The line between fiction and real life is very thin indeed.

2 SEXUALITY AT THE EDGE OF THE ABYSS: the Marquis de Sade

VIRTUALLY nothing that can be said about sexuality and erotic experience cannot be found in the extensive writings of the Marquis de Sade. For better or for worse, he is the primary author in any study of sexual fiction. We have only begun to appreciate the range and intensity of his sexual imagination. Like Freud later, Sade understood that there is no human experience that is not colored by the workings of the libido and the id. And both Sade and Freud are profoundly anti-romantic writers. Sexual compulsions are part of the tragic, limited, fallible condition of man – the same pessimistic assumptions from which existential philosophers begin – doomed to endless repetitions that can never satisfy the ideal images of the spirit. There is nothing that reminds man more of his precarious metaphysical situation than sex, and it is not surprising that 'death', 'dying', 'little death' should be words for orgasm both in English and in European languages. Sade's somber view of man, utterly cut off from God and any religious or philosophical consolation, seems very relevant to modern currents of thought, especially in France.

Sade is a completely naturalistic philosopher. He worships nature in place of God. Not the beneficent and healing nature of Rousseau, but rather the nature who is Edmund's goddess in *King Lear*: powerful, brutal, amoral, the center of chaos by which the strong dominate the weak. Nature sanctions pure egoism in every man and woman, thus suggesting an implicit survival of the fittest. In sexual matters each individual strives to fulfill himself or herself without regard to anyone else. There is no mutuality, reciprocity or love. The strong take their overpowering pleasure at the expense of the weak. It is not surprising that in Sade sexual fulfillment comes through pain, oppression, torture and victimization. What we now call 'sadism' is essential to Sade's metaphysical and political system, although torturer and victim are surprisingly linked in what seem reversible, sadomasochistic rituals.

In Sade sexuality is always placed in a communal, group setting. It is not a solitary activity, but a public enactment of libertine values. Sex is theatricalized in Sade, and the orgy is his most natural form of sexual experience. Individual pleasure seems to have little to do with it; if it is pleasure, it is a hysterical, frenzied and excruciating pleasure that has no connection with hedonistic enjoyment. Everything is done with wild excess in Sade, and sexuality becomes a vehicle for the demonstration of philosophical points. When a bout of feverish and cruel sex has been completed, Sade's powerful heroes discuss the kinds of questions that preoccupied the Enlightenment philosophers in eighteenth-century France. They conduct their own salons exclusively devoted to sexuality in theory and practice. The sex seems to be a necessary prelude to clear everyone's mind of lustful and materialistic thoughts. In its turn, the discussion then stimulates further sexual encounters. It is an endless dualism. Quite clearly these alternating scenes are being played out in the author's mind. Sade was extraordinarily prolific; although a good deal of his work has been lost, thousands of pages still remain. He wrote in a kind of masturbatory frenzy, especially in prison, where he spent at least twenty-eight years (and most of his adult life).

Sade was bitterly opposed to the optimistic and benevolent view of nature – that of the 'noble savage' – found in Rousseau. Sade does not believe in the natural goodness of man. In many ways he shares the Calvinist conviction of natural depravity. In a state of nature man follows his egoistic instincts. He strives to maximize his own pleasure and satisfaction without regard to the interests of his fellow creatures. Although Sade had much in common with Hobbes, especially in his conception of the state of nature, Sade never postulated a contract theory for the origin of human society. Why would the most powerful want to surrender their power for some greater good? Didn't the greatest good consist in their own self-fulfillment? There is no benevolence or social concern in Sade's view of nature.

In *Justine* (1791), Coeur-de-fer specifically rejects any notion of a social contract behind civil society:

> All men are born isolated, envious, cruel and despotic; wishing to have everything and surrender nothing, incessantly struggling to maintain either their rights or achieve their ambition, the legislator comes up and says to them: Cease thus to fight; if each were to retreat a little, calm would be restored. I find no fault with the position implicit in the agreement, but I maintain that two species of individuals cannot and ought not to submit to it, ever; those who feel they are the stronger have no need to give up anything in order to be happy, and those who find themselves the weaker also find themselves giving up infinitely more than what is assured them. (p. 494)

Society is ruled by power relations, and Sade's mighty heroes are always surprisingly intelligent, articulate, self-aware and therefore ruthless. In both *Justine* and *Philosophy in the Bedroom* (1795), from which we shall draw many of our examples, there are both endless self-explanation and self-justification.

In sexual matters the law of nature is to follow your own impulses without regard to the needs of others. All sex in Sade is a form of tyranny, by which the dominant partner imposes his will on the subservient sex object. All relations are sadomasochistic ones, with the possibility that the roles can be temporarily changed for purposes of experimentation, but there still remains a fundamental distinction between master and slave, between the active and the passive partner. Thus sexual activity in Sade always has a strongly

masturbatory character, since mutuality between the partners has been rigorously excluded. The passive partner is
merely the vessel in which the active partner fulfills himself.
As the cruel and villainous Clément expresses it to his captive audience in *Justine*:

> If egoism is Nature's fundamental commandment, it is
> very surely most of all during our lubricious delights that
> this celestial Mother desires us to be most absolutely
> under its rule; why, it's a very small evil, is it not, that, in
> the interests of the augmentation of the man's lecherous
> delights he has got either to neglect or upset the woman's;
> for if this upsetting of her pleasure causes him to gain
> any, what is lost to the object which serves him affects him
> in no wise, save profitably: it must be a matter of indiffer-
> ence to him whether that object is happy or unhappy,
> provided it be delectable to him; in truth, there is no
> relation at all between that object and himself. (p. 604)

The last phrase is the heart of the matter: 'there is no
relation at all between that object and himself'. Thus sex is
a purely instrumental and demonstrative activity. It is
designed not only to give pleasure to the master, but also to
show his absolute power over his sex object. One wonders
why Sade's villains have such a compulsive and seemingly
infinite need to explain themselves and to justify themselves
in the most rational and abstruse terms. If they indeed felt
the powers that they postulate, they would not dissipate
them in such elaborate discourse. It seems as if Sade's vil-
lain/heroes protest too much because they suffer from *la
mauvaise conscience*.

This rationalizing element makes Sade's libertine
philosophy so different from other libertine literature.
While virtually every sexual combination imaginable is set
forth in Sade's works, there is also a paucity of lubricious
detail. Sade's gargantuan sexual imagination is not intended
to provoke or inflame desire; rather the vast repetition has a
numbing effect. We feel disgust and outrage much more
vividly than desire. Sade speaks of the sexual impulse,
physiologically, as an irritation that must be gotten rid of by

any means in order for a person to maintain his health. It is a sudden mania that comes upon its subject like a dark cloud, a temporary fit of insanity, an indulgence of whim and caprice at any cost. Once the fit is past, Sade's characters are once again civil, gracious, sensitive, cultivated and articulate human beings.

Sexuality is thus a form of debasement for both subject and object, and Sade's sexual attitudes are closely connected with his atheism: in both, what is important is sacrilege, blasphemy, insult, as if both atheism and sexual indulgence were negative and demonic forces in which one seeks to immerse oneself and also perhaps to immolate oneself. Going all the way in atheism and sex implies a deliberateness, an intensity that grows out of intellectual conviction rather than psychological motivation. In a primitive sense Sade wants to be evil, as a small child wants to be bad, in order to call attention to himself and to test authority. There is something infantile in Sade's grandiose visions of orgies and religious desecrations. He is always calling upon God, if he exists, to punish him as he so richly deserves, and in fact it is the absence of any response that throws Sade into metaphysical despair.

Pain and cruelties and tortures are necessary in order to assure the libertine that he is alive. They are public demonstrations of sexuality. Most of Sade's heroes would be impotent without enacting melodramatic scenes of punishment. The Count de Gernande, for example, with whom the compassionate Justine is more than a little in love, is physically prepubescent:

> It was then I noticed, not without astonishment, that this giant, this species of monster whose aspect alone was enough to strike terror, was howbeit barely a man; the most meager, the most minuscule excrescence of flesh or, to make a juster comparison, what one might find in a child of three was all one discovered upon this so very enormous and otherwise so corpulent individual . . . . Such was his satiety, such his impotence that the extrem-

est efforts availed not at all, and he remained in his torpor. (p. 641)

Justine is always remarkably observant, especially of sexual details. Her absolute innocence gives her license to see all and do all (more properly, have all done to her) without complicity. Pain is a stimulus to jaded sexual appetites, but more importantly it functions in Sade as the reality principle. It is the moment of truth when torturer and tortured encounter each other, and the torturer needs the right sort of victim in order for his pleasure to be fulfilled.

Sade is continually talking of pain as a stimulus to the intellect. As Madame de Saint-Ange explains it to Eugénie, her 15-year-old disciple in *Philosophy in the Bedroom*:

> May atrocities, horrors, may the most odious crimes astonish you no more, my Eugénie; what is of the filthiest, the most infamous, the most forbidden, 'tis that which best rouses the intellect . . . 'tis that which always causes us most deliciously to discharge. (p. 233)

What does Sade mean by 'intellect'? It seems to mean 'imagination', in the sense that a keen imagination may apprehend and understand with special acuity the reality presented to it. To Sade pain is a natural, deeply-seated, primitive emotion that can be documented both biologically and anthropologically. It is inherent in all living things, both men and animals, to inflict pain; the argument from nature is overwhelming:

> The infant breaks his toy, bites his nurse's breast, strangles his canary long before he is able to reason; cruelty is stamped in animals, in whom, as I think I have said, Nature's laws are more emphatically to be read than in ourselves; cruelty exists among savages, so much nearer to Nature than civilized men are; absurd then to maintain cruelty is a consequence of depravity. I repeat, the doctrine is false. Cruelty is natural. . . . Cruelty is simply the energy in a man civilization has not yet altogether corrupted: therefore it is a virtue, not a vice. (pp. 253–4)

This is aggressively anti-Rousseau in its somber vision of civilization corrupting man's natural energies. Cruelty, and especially cruelty in sex, has a vitality in danger of extinction.

These are alarming paradoxes, but Sade at least recognizes a primitive mystery in the sexual relation that is more puzzling than the rather tepid spiritual union being proclaimed by his contemporaries. Sade is a spokesman for hard and difficult sex, violent, cruel and energetic. Orgasm unites man with the animal creation and is a kind of epileptic fit or temporary seizure by which we abandon all pretensions to reason and false enlightenment. Against a benevolent and optimistic romanticism, Sade opposes a negative, primitive, chaotic and destructive view of the sexual relation. 'There is not a living man who does not wish to play the despot when he is stiff,' says Dolmancé (p. 344), the most depraved character in *Philosophy in the Bedroom* and therefore, supposedly, modeled on Sade himself. Between bouts of ingenious group sex, Dolmancé leads the equally ingenious discussion of erotic philosophy:

> Would pleasure's climax be a kind of fury were it not the intention of this mother of humankind that behaviour during copulation be the same as behavior in anger? What well-made man, in a word, what man endowed with vigorous organs does not desire, in one fashion or in another, to molest his partner during his enjoyment of her? (p. 345)

Molesting your partner is apparently an expression of 'the energy in a man civilization has not yet altogether corrupted'. Sade's lovers are characteristically wild men whose passions cannot be restrained. Nature is used in a circular way to justify whatever impulses the libertine feels – it is his religion – yet at other times nature is deprived of its normative qualities. Is the libertine obeying the dictates of nature, or is he himself an uncontrollable natural force? There is an important distinction between these two positions.

Sade flirts with crime as the final expression of unrestrained, naturalistic sensuality. *The 120 Days of Sodom* (1785) has an elaborate catalogue of the 150 criminal passions (Part 3) followed by the 150 murderous passions (Part 4). These sections were never written out, so that the summary statements have a certain macabre/comic quality, like a repertory of Grand Guignol plots. Thus number 30 in Part 3 is a scenario for a little Gothic tale:

> *He fucks a turkey whose head is gripped between the legs of a girl lying on her belly — while in action he looks quite as if he were embuggering the girl. While he is at work he is being sodomized, and the moment he discharges, the girl cuts the turkey's throat.* (p. 603)

The next fantasy is equally extravagant:

> *He fucks a goat from behind while being flogged; the goat conceives and gives birth to a monster. Monster though it be, he embuggers it.* (p. 603)

These samples read like a catalogue of erotic folklore rather than a chamber of horrors.

The book has a certain Arabian Nights quality, since the story-tellers in Part I (which is fully written) dominate the action. The narrations have a strong thematic influence on the orgies that follow, but the orgies seem more like the realization of the fictions than independent events in their own right. The whole of *The 120 Days of Sodom* thus distances the outrages by setting them in a fictional, story-telling context. It is a remarkably ambitious, copious and encyclopedic work, with four separate month-long narrations each consisting of 150 passions (simple, complex, criminal and murderous). Sade is trying to include every conceivable aspect of sexuality in his complete system. Why does it need to be so complete? Sade writes compulsively to fill up all blanks and to produce a masterpiece of sexual knowledge that can rival the French *Encyclopédie*, which had been completed about ten years earlier. *The 120 Days of Sodom* turns out to be much more a vast anthology of sexual motifs than a compendium of human knowledge. It is in many ways

Sade's most daring book. The very idea that all of human experience can be universalized and categorized under 600 sexual passions is itself extraordinarily original.

Sade is constantly returning to the tabooed idea that murder is the ultimate and logical expression of sexual energies. This is the test case for his profoundly negative philosophy of nature, since he has grandiose, apocalyptic visions of destroying himself along with all other human beings and cutting off any further possibility of human life. The great atomic war of science fiction would seem to Sade the ultimate orgasm, especially in its image of one final explosion that brings on the end of the world. The sexual image is tainted with religious overtones, and Sade delights in playing a cruel, lustful, arbitrary and completely destructive God. Near the end of *Justine* (when many less titillating devices have already been exhausted), the ferocious Roland toys with the idea of being hanged – or coming as close to it as possible – in order to experience the deliciously voluptuous sensations of the moment just before death. He first experiments with Justine, then tries it himself:

> This torture is sweeter than you may imagine . . . you will only approach death by way of unspeakably pleasurable sensations; the pressure this noose will bring to bear upon your nervous system will set fire to the organs of voluptuousness; the effect is certain; were all the people who are condemned to this torture to know in what an intoxication of joy it makes one die, less terrified by this retribution for their crimes, they would commit them more often and with much greater self-assurance. (p. 675)

Nagisa Oshima uses this ecstatic death for the male hero of his film, *In the Realm of the Senses,* after the wildly obsessive lovers have worn each other out. In a final erotic frenzy they play with longer and longer stranglings until death occurs quietly and effortlessly. It is frightening for the audience to participate in the literal, physical *Liebestod.* As in Bo Widerberg's *Elvira Madigan* there is no other logical way for the movie to end. The deaths become a 'consummation devoutly to be wished'.

Although there are some remarkably powerful women in Sade, especially in *Juliette* (1797), the counter-novel to *Justine*, Sade's women are generally subservient to men. They are always conscious of living in a man's world, and even if they succeed through cunning and ruthlessness, like some of the old whores in *The 120 Days of Sodom*, their success depends upon knowing how to please men. No matter how skillful and insightful some women may be as players, the rules of the game are set by men. Sade pays lip-service to the absolute freedom of women, but he also finds abundant examples everywhere about him to demonstrate that, by nature, women are the weaker sex and therefore born to serve male needs.

There is a certain ambiguity about this point that Sade cannot resolve. Like modern proselytizers for the new feminist biology (such as Mary Jane Sherfey and Barbara Seaman), Sade understands that women have greater sexual capacity than men and therefore a more pressing need for sexual freedom:

> I say then that women, having been endowed with considerably more violent penchants for carnal pleasure than we, will be able to give themselves over to it wholeheartedly, absolutely free of all encumbering hymeneal ties, of all false notions of modesty, absolutely restored to a state of Nature; I want laws permitting them to give themselves to as many men as they see fit; I would have them accorded the enjoyment of all sexes and, as in the case of men, the enjoyment of all parts of the body; and under the special clause prescribing their surrender to all who desire them, there must be subjoined another guaranteeing them a similar freedom to enjoy all they deem worthy to satisfy them. (p. 321)

The last stipulation is startling, since it would imply that women have the same freedom to subjugate men to their needs as men have to prostitute women. This freedom postulates an exact equality between men and women, but in fact it is illusory, because one's rights depend ultimately on the ability to enforce them. Even in a civil society men can dominate women by physical force. The revolutionary utopia envisaged in 'Yet Another Effort, Frenchmen, If You Would Become Republicans', which is included in the fifth dialogue of *Philosophy in the Bedroom*, has no inherent rights at all. By its institutions society should facilitate the sexual enslavement of women by men, although it is up to the men to claim their own prerogatives. There is no real sexual equality or democracy in this utopia, no matter how much Sade may need these admirable beliefs to round out his argument.

The feminist (or pseudo-feminist) argument is best pursued in *Philosophy in the Bedroom*, which is literally an educational dialogue intended to induct the 15-year-old Eugénie de Mistival into the libertine philosophy. Dolmancé enunciates the basic premise for the young ingenue: ' 'tis, in a word, to be fucked that you were born', but he continues in a style that is more ominous: 'and . . . she who refuses her obedience to this intention Nature has for her does not deserve to see the light longer' (p. 267). We know that Dolmancé is not accustomed to making idle threats. He is a committed libertine, not a casual hedonist, and his instructions to Eugénie have a quality of religious and aesthetic fervor:

> O voluptuous young women, deliver your bodies unto us as often and as much as you wish! Fuck, divert yourselves, that's the essential thing; but be quick to fly from love. . . . Women are not made for one single man; 'tis for men at large Nature created them. Listening only to this sacred voice, let them surrender themselves, indifferently, to all who want them: always whores, never mistresses, eschewing love, worshiping pleasure. (pp. 285–6)

Love is, of course, an entirely negative quality in Sade; it is a form of possessiveness that denies a natural egoism and tries to make a property of the loved one. In being a whore, a woman is asserting both her natural freedom and function.

This is the same doctrine that Madame de Saint-Ange preaches: 'Woman's destiny is to be wanton, like the bitch, the she-wolf; she must belong to all who claim her. Clearly, it is to outrage the fate Nature imposes upon women to fetter them by the absurd ties of a solitary marriage' (p. 219). Madame de Saint-Ange is an early proponent of open marriage.

In the ideal society of 'Yet Another Effort, Frenchmen . . .', Sade projects an elaborate system of enforced prostitution for women that has little to do with any choice on their part about fulfilling their carnal nature. Women can be summoned at any time, by those males who desire them, to special houses in the city where their summoners are permitted to act out all of their impulses no matter how cruel or how extreme:

> A man who would like to enjoy whatever woman or girl will henceforth be able, if the laws you promulgate are just, to have her summoned at once to duty at one of the houses; and there, under the supervision of the matrons of that temple of Venus, she will be surrendered to him, to satisfy, humbly and with submission, all the fancies in which he will be pleased to indulge with her, however strange or irregular they may be, since there is no extravagance which is not in Nature, none which she does not acknowledge as her own. (p. 320)

This is a classic male fantasy, usually adolescent, of having sexual power over all the women one meets, including strangers on crowded streets or subway cars. Sade's word, 'irregular', is a euphemism for kinky sex, and the whole passage is ornamented with the quasi-legal language of utopian planning.

Behind the innocuous formulations of political theory lies the threat of force. It may well be true that women, in a state of nature, 'are born *vulquivaguous*, that is to say, are born enjoying the advantages of other female animals and belonging, like them and without exception, to all males' (p. 318), but if women refuse to acknowledge their

vulquivaguousness, 'we have the right to compel their submission' (p. 319). This is the final argument that invigorates
all the others:

> It cannot be denied that we have the right to decree laws
> that compel woman to yield to the flames of him who
> would have her; violence itself being one of that right's
> effects, we can employ it lawfully. Indeed! has Nature not
> proven that we have that right, by bestowing upon us the
> strength needed to bend women to our will? (p. 319)

This is charmingly illogical in a way characteristic of Sade.
Nature both discovers truth and also promotes irrationality
by allowing force to triumph over truth. Nature cannot be at
one and the same time a system of values and a punitive
system for enforcing those values. By setting up a utopian
society founded on law, Sade seems to be forgetting his own
profound conviction that brute force can make its own laws.

Did Sade hate women? It is true that his works are full of
the wildest misogyny. The blood-letting Count de Gernande
in *Justine* unleashes a tirade about the natural inferiority of
all women:

> A puny creature, always inferior to man, infinitely less
> attractive than he is, less ingenious, less wise, constructed
> in a disgusting manner entirely opposite to what is cap-
> able of pleasing a man, to what is able to delight him . . . a
> being three-quarters of her life untouchable, unwhole-
> some, unable to satisfy her mate throughout the entire
> period Nature constrains her to childbearing, of a sharp
> turn of humor, shrill, shrewish, bitter, and thwart; a
> tyrant if you allow her privileges, mean, vile, and a sneak
> in bondage; always false, forever mischievous, constantly
> dangerous; in short, a being so perverse that during
> several convocations the question was very soberly agi-
> tated at the Council of Mâcon whether or not this pecu-
> liar creature, as distinct from man as is man from the ape,
> had any reasonably legitimate pretensions to classifica-
> tion as a human. (p. 647)

The hatred of women is so rabid in this passage that Gernande seems to be taking his revenge against the entire sex by phlebotomizing his wife at regular intervals.

Yet women and the feminine sensibility play a crucial role in interpreting reality in Sade's works. Both *Justine* and *Juliette* are written from the point of view of a woman, and all the stories in *The 120 Days of Sodom* are told by women. Sade's heroes may scorn the genital areas of women – the seat of nature – but they bugger women with great ardor and enthusiasm, and strictly homosexual relations are considered ancillary to heterosexual intercourse. There is a great deal of bisexual activity in Sade's works, yet his own sexuality remains ambiguous. Women encourage the kind of profound guilt feelings that he can take pleasure in overcoming. They are the animating force of Sade's sexual fantasy, as Angela Carter understands so well in her ingenious book, *The Sadeian Woman*. Justine's virginal passivity and Juliette's sexual terror combine essential aspects of Sade's curious feminism. Woman becomes an awesome projection of male fears and male rage – the paradoxically double image of the sadomasochistic imagination.

There is a peculiarly mental quality about Sade's sexual fantasies. Their realism is never meant to be convincing because there is such a paucity of authentic details, either physical or sociological, or simply of the sense of daily life that so many novelists manage to convey. Sade's fictions present a world apart. In *Justine* the usual settings are a forest, a castle, a dungeon. The male villain/heroes are impossibly rich and resourceful, which facilitates their omnipotence in the face of the poor and friendless Justine. But Justine is much more implicated psychologically in the action than is at first apparent. Although she lends herself wonderfully well to be the much abused heroine, she is constantly reasoning with and haranguing her tormentors. They begin to need her in order to have someone interesting to talk to, and they pretend to repentances they have no intention of fulfilling in order to retain her sympathetic company. In the midst of cruel and unimaginable slaughters, Justine has a wonderful facility for staying alive. She is cunning at self-preservation, and she very subtly becomes a fictional character by her ingenuity and fortitude. Against cruel extravagance, she opposes a powerful common sense.

Justine becomes subtly involved in her own adventures, no matter how horrible, and she usually falls in love with her inhuman but dashing and manly tormentor. She confesses openly to her infatuation with the vicious Comte de Bressac:

> Whatever the foul treatment to which the Comte de Bressac had exposed me the first day I had met him, it had, all the same, been impossible to see him so frequently without feeling myself drawn toward him by an insuperable and instinctive tenderness. Despite all my recollections of his cruelty, all my thoughts upon his disinclinations toward women, upon the depravity of his tastes, upon the gulf which separated us morally, nothing in the world was able to extinguish this nascent passion, and had the Count called upon me to lay down my life, I would have sacrificed it for him a thousand times over. (p. 511)

So Justine is not so completely a moral creature as she pretends to be; she has a definite emotional stake in the action and is filled with the profound ambivalence of Richardson's Pamela.

Towards the monstrous Comte de Bressac, she is the romantic heroine torn by her obligations to honor and to passion:

> I trembled; I beheld this conduct with horror. I strove to rationalize my reactions by attributing their origin to personal motives, for I wished to stifle the unhappy passion which burned in my soul; but is love an illness to be cured? All I endeavored to oppose to it merely fanned its flames, and the perfidious Count never appeared more lovable to me than when I had assembled before me everything which ought to have induced me to hate him. (p. 517)

Justine is caught in the classic war between the values of the head and the heart, and this, of course, renders her ineffective as an antagonist and incapacitates her from abandoning her tyrannous masters.

In a typical stance, Justine plays the role of missionary and strives to convert the moral monsters into whose clutches she has fallen. Presumably if she can persuade them to change their evil ways, her love can be fulfilled, and the happy ending is on its way – not the bolt of lightning which actually destroys Justine after she is finally rescued from all of her tormentors. To Roland, the child-abuser and savage whipper who is determined to sacrifice his daughter in the interests of science, Justine offers herself as spiritual consoler; Roland implores her not to forsake him:

> Ah, Thérèse [Justine's assumed name], remain with me, stay here, Thérèse, my child, it will be a joy to have you; in the midst of the many vices to which I am driven by a fiery temper, an unrestrainable imagination and a much rotted heart, at least I will have the comfort of a virtuous being dwelling close by, and upon whose breast I shall be able to cast myself as at the feet of a God when, glutted by my debauches. . . . . (p. 543)

This is as close as Roland ever comes to spiritual confession, but his contrition goes no further. He needs Justine, as everyone in Southern and Hoffenberg's novel needs Candy.

Nowhere is Justine in a greater dilemma than with the Count de Gernande, who can only experience orgasm by seeing his wife's blood spurting from her arms. While this is occurring, Justine is busily fellating the Count:

> For my part, certain that the instant at which the hoped for crisis occurs will bring a conclusion to the Countess' torments, I bring all my efforts to bear upon precipitating this denouement, and I become, as, Madame, you observe, I become a whore from kindness, a libertine through virtue . . . he wishes to fly at his wife, I restrain him: I pump the last drop from him, his need of me

makes him respect me; at last I bring him to his senses by ridding him of that fiery liquid, whose heat, whose viscosity, and above all whose abundance puts him in such a frenzy I believe he is going to expire. (p. 643)

What could be more appealing in Justine than to combine vigorous fellatio with equally animated moral discourse? Thus she has it all ways at once: she protects the Countess, she restrains the Count and she makes love therapeutically and without guilt. In the ultimate sexual paradox, she is a 'whore from kindness, a libertine through virtue'. These psychological touches in the presentation of Justine show us novelistic possibilities that Sade could have exploited further but didn't. He is generally content to pursue Justine's adventures as a moral fable rather than a novel.

We can never escape the postulated and propositional character of Sade's tales. As we have seen, *The 120 Days of Sodom* is laid out with excessive fullness, regularity and symmetry. Everything is so balanced against everything else that the massive equilibrium weighs us down. It is a fable of order superimposed on the wild chaos of its sexual subject. Central to the fiction is the fantasy of a world apart, a Gothic castle lost to the world, hidden, impregnable, self-sufficient, where everything is permitted. There are no restraints of any kind. The Benedictine monastery of St Mary-in-the-Wood in *Justine* is an attempt to reproduce the more elaborately described German castle of Silling in *The 120 Days of Sodom*, the manuscript of which Sade believed was forever lost in the sacking of the Bastille (it was rediscovered and first published in 1931–5) and which Sade tried to rewrite in *Juliette*.

The opening address of the Duc de Blangis to his captive crew at Silling sets the tone for understanding the narrative. Everyone has disappeared off the face of the earth, both tormentors and victims alike. At Silling they are enacting another mode of existence that has no relation to their ordinary lives:

Give a thought to your circumstances, think what you are,

what we are, and may these reflections cause you to quake – you are beyond the borders of France in the depths of an uninhabitable forest, high amongst naked mountains; the paths that brought you here were destroyed behind you as you advanced along them. You are enclosed in an impregnable citadel; no one on earth knows you are here, you are beyond the reach of your friends, of your kin: insofar as the world is concerned, you are already dead, and if yet you breathe, 'tis by our pleasure, and for it only. (pp. 250–1)

This is the basic postulate of Gothic fiction, and once this is understood everyone is more comfortable. All the characters live only in their communal sexual life, and all reality is reduced to its sexual component. As in *My Secret Life*, everything becomes suffocatingly sexual in *The 120 Days of Sodom*. The exclusive preoccupation with sex assures us that, 'insofar as the world is concerned', the characters 'are already dead'. As in so many Poe stories, death is imagined as a womb-like state of being buried alive.

In both Silling and St Mary-in-the-Wood we are oppressed by the fullness and elaborateness of the rules by which everyone lives. The lewd monks in *Justine* are rigid in their detailed codification of all possible laws and their specific punishments. As Omphale shrewdly observes to Justine,

> not that the libertines need all that in order to vent their fury upon us, but they welcome excuses; the look of legitimacy that may be given to a piece of viciousness renders it more agreeable in their eyes, adds to its piquancy, its charm. (p. 582)

The 'look of legitimacy' is the fundamental illusion. It is also a fundamental irony, since the societies of *Justine* and *The 120 Days of Sodom* are lawless and illegitimate by their very nature. But the laws establish artificial restraints. At Silling, for example, no one can deflower the virgins until a set time, and heavy fines are introduced, even for the four principals, for any infraction of these historical stipulations.

Although *The 120 Days of Sodom* was never completed – it would have been at least 1200 pages, if we multiply the 300 pages of Part I by four – we understand from the plan that the passions grow more serious and more criminal as the narrative progresses. The characters too gradually become debased by their debaucheries, so that at the end we find them engaged in randomly homicidal actions that would have been inconceivable at the beginning. This deterioration is omitted from the much shorter episode of St Mary-in-the-Wood in *Justine*.

Sade depends upon large effects, vast scenarios, endless repetitions and recombinations. His work is essentially circular because there is no conceivable ending. Sexuality can only be fulfilled temporarily and approximately; it can never achieve the apotheosis of a heavenly vision, that need only be revealed once and for all time. It is to Sade's great merit as an author that he links sex so strongly to the powers of the imagination. Thus the frenzied and vicious monk, Clément, once his lust has been momentarily sated, can discourse with Justine with sweet reasonableness on the theme that 'objects have no value for us save that which our imagination imparts to them':

> Now, if we admit that the senses' joy is always dependent upon the imagination, always regulated by the imagination, one must not be amazed by the numerous variations the imagination is apt to suggest during the pleasurable episode, by the infinite multitude of different tastes and passions the imagination's various extravagances will bring to light. (p. 601)

As a good Freudian, Clément understands that many of our imaginative predilections are either innate or are established in early childhood:

> It is in the mother's womb that there are fashioned the organs which must render us susceptible of such-and-such a fantasy; the first objects which we encounter, the first conversations we overhear determine the pattern;

once tastes are formed nothing in the world can destroy them. (p. 601)

In Sade's vision man is responsible for his own irrationality and strives to fulfill himself although he knows that he is doomed to failure. There is a hypnotic re-enactment of this failure throughout his works, in which actor and sufferer, active and passive, master and slave, are joined in some vast circle. The tormenter needs his victim in order to complete his own being, and his own sexuality is the ultimate torment of the tormentor. Despite their frenzied activity, the characters are oppressed by the meaninglessness of existence. They have been deserted by God the Father, and they flee in terror from the mother with whom they are locked in guilty incest. There is no comfort to be found in any philosophical or religious system. They understand their own boredom, isolation and impending death. Sex becomes a frantic and desperate way of asserting their being in a world without values. In its purely physical, involuntary excitement, sex offers an illusory, fragmentary and disappointing proof that the characters are alive. As Angela Carter puts it so well, Sade 'cites the flesh as existential verification in itself, in a rewriting of the Cartesian cogito: *"I fuck therefore I am"*' (p. 26).

3 EROTIC SAINTHOOD AND THE SEARCH FOR SELF-ANNIHILATION: *Story of O* and *The Image*

P AULINE Réage's *Story of O* (1954) and Jean de Berg's *The Image* (1956) are both extraordinary pastiches – almost parodies – of the kinds of sadomasochistic scenes, characters and paraphernalia we find so often in the pages of Sade. The Divine Marquis is by no means subtle, so that writers in the same tradition seem even more blatant and theatrical. The mysteriously pseudonymous Pauline Réage and Jean de Berg, who may conceivably be the same person, acknowledge no debt to Sade, and in fact in Pauline Réage's preface to *Return to the Château* (1969), a composition made up of parts edited out of *Story of O*, the author claims to have encountered Sade only later in her life:

> So it was that Sade's castles, discovered long after I had silently built my own, never surprised me. . . . But Sade made me understand that we are all jailers, and all in prison, in that there is always someone within us whom we enchain, whom we imprison, whom we silence. By a curious kind of reverse shock, it can happen that prison itself can open the gates to freedom. (pp. 11–12)

The prison metaphor is especially apt for Sade, who spent so much of his adult life in various prisons. Pauline Réage seems also to owe a heavy debt to Dostoevsky and his compassionate belief in the enlightenment that comes only through suffering.

Both *Story of O* and *The Image* are highly formalized and

ritualized books. We are only on the periphery of an external life in the real world, since both books distinguish between an inner circle of initiates into a sexual mystery and an outer circle of the imperceptive and disbelieving world. The initiates are part of a secret society with its own rules, its own values and its own lifestyle. In this society time seems to have stopped. Everything happens in an eternal present, and the characters have only the most shadowy past. In another life both O and Claire apparently earn their living as fashion photographers, but both novels progressively abandon any links with a practical, material, money-grubbing world. What does Sir Stephen do for a living? It is only in *Return to the Château* that we learn some tantalizing details: he is Scottish, a member of the Campbell clan (although he is everywhere described as an English lord), he is involved in international finance, perhaps in diamond mines in the Congo, since he apparently kills Carl, who wants to take O away from Roissy. These are all meaningless details of Gothic fiction and have no real bearing on the novel, which is deliberately static, non-referential and ahistorical. Everything occurs as if in a dream.

As in Antonioni's movie *Blow-Up* (based on a story by Julio Cortázar), photography serves as a characteristic metaphor for the displacement of reality in *Story of O* and especially in *The Image*. The line that separates the real world from the photographed images of it is intentionally blurred. The aesthetic dimension is also the erotic dimension, as the real world of everyday life is seen frozen in a certain moment of light, color and mass in the photograph. The persons are stripped of their complex, pulsating, psychological life and made to seem like objects. There is an intense concentration on effect, and both people and objects become magical, fetishistic. The moment recorded in the photograph is completely out of context, it is abstracted, and it is radically transformed from what it might have been in its own continuum. By speaking of the aesthetic quality of photographs, we also, at the same time, seem to be speaking about erotic fantasy, which acts by exclusion, by concentration and by the elaboration of images evoked by very limited and static materials.

Chapter 5 of *The Image* is, in fact, called 'The photographs'. The man in the story, Jean de Berg, examines a series of sadomasochistic pictures of Anne, made by Claire. His commentary is laced with the professional jargon of someone who understands the art of photography, yet the images are strangely brought to life by the viewer. He endows them with a kind of life they could not possibly have in themselves, especially the photograph showing Anne with 'two deep wounds from which blood flows freely':

> One extends from the tip of the breast to the armpit, on the side where there are no ropes. The blood pours down one whole side in little rivers of varying force which run together and separate again in an elaborate network which covers one hip and a good part of the stomach. It even flows into the navel and the pubic hair in a thick stream which runs down the belly. (p. 70)

It is worth noting that the pouring of the blood and its thick stream is surely a cinematic detail that could not be discerned in a photograph. The effect of this animation is to transform the two-dimensional image into a vivid, theatricalized scene.

The description of the second wound intensifies the emotional effect:

> The second wound, in the lower part of the body, ornaments the other side. It pierces the groin just above the pubis, penetrating the lower belly and curving down to the inner part of the thigh. The blood from this wound flows in large rivers, almost covering the whole area, running down to the rope which binds the body above the knees. There it accumulates a moment and then pours out directly onto one of the white flagstones where a pool has formed. (pp. 70–1)

Everything in the detailed account of the picture suggests a painting rather than a photograph, particularly a Baroque rendering of the Crucifixion. The language is deliberately simplified and stripped of any emotive words, but this only heightens the effect. Notice that the second wound 'ornaments' the first. The blood flows 'in large rivers', but the viewer is interested in the scene only as an aesthetic composition. He does not venture to comment on the human subject.

The climax of this chapter is the anomalous photograph that Claire presents to Jean at the end of the series:

> She handed it to me. Right away I could tell that it was different from the others. The way it was taken, in the first place, was not at all the same, but there were other things. The body was partially cut off by the camera, while before it had always been shown in its entirety. The setting, moreover, was no longer the austere Gothic room but the very room that we were sitting in. Thrown back in one of the little armchairs a woman, her nightgown raised to her waist, is caressing the interior of her sex. (p. 73)

This picture of Claire masturbating is intended of course as a sexual invitation, but, like Marcher in Henry James's story, 'The Beast in the Jungle' (1903), Jean doesn't understand the woman's initiatives. The lewd photograph of Claire functions as a slice of life inappropriately interpolated into a scene where it cannot have its proper meaning. The author teases us with sexual ironies about what is real and what is merely represented. The images are luridly animated, while the persons remain aloofly critical and intellectual.

In the scene in the Bagatelle Gardens, Anne glides through the setting like a photographer's model or beautiful doll/puppet, who needs to be animated by Claire in even the minutest gestures. The action is static and frozen because Anne is deprived of human volition. She is an object: a sex object, a photographer's object, a lost doll – it hardly matters. The scenes are composed for their picturability:

> Anne held her right hand out toward the half-opened flower. Very gently she ran her finger tips around the

outer edges of the petals, partly closed, barely touching
their tender pink flesh. She ran her fingers several times
around the closed heart, very slowly. Then she delicately
spread open the inner petals and closed them again,
using all five fingers. (p. 32)

The rose as vulva echoes comparable tropical scenes in
Anaïs Nin's *Delta of Venus*. Anne is dehumanized in order to
enact sexual symbolism for Jean and Claire. When Anne is
directed to put a rose (with thorny stem) under her garter
belt, Claire contemplates her 'like a connoisseur appraising
a painting' (p. 42). By ceasing to be human, Anne becomes
an erotic art object.

Although O is a fashion photographer, photography as
an art enters less significantly into *Story of O* than it does in
The Image, yet in both novels there is a sense of stasis, of an
aesthetic silence and composition in the material world, of a
distanced, pictorial and highly formalized reality that has its
roots in painting and photography. Seeing O as a photographer does not give us any new insights into her real life,
but only corroborates her obsessional, secret life with René,
Sir Stephen and the enclosed world of Roissy. Jacqueline,
the model, becomes O's alter ego, as O seems to see herself
posed in an elaborate, antiquated costume:

> she was wearing an enormous robe of heavy brocaded
> silk, red like the dress of a bride in the Middle Ages,
> which came down to below her ankles, flared at the hips
> and tight at the waist, and the armature of which traced
> the outline of her bosom. It was what the dress designers
> called a gala gown, the kind no one ever wears. The
> spike-heeled sandals were also of red silk. (p. 62)

Although Jacqueline mimics the costume of Roissy, she is
put into the novel to be a counter-figure to O. When she
removes her gala gown, Jacqueline becomes a human entity
again, who wants to be alone in her dressing room. The
costume never becomes a part of her life, as it does with O,
who is progressively dehumanized into an art object, a cos-

tumed enacter of roles, like that of the owl in the final sequence.

There is a great deal of deliberate archaizing in *Story of O*. The narrative is simplified, and the style is highly reminiscent of an eighteenth-century *conte* in the style of Voltaire. Everything is stripped down and displaced. The author cultivates an effect of distance and distancing. If we are still in the twentieth century, the narrative has been slowed down and abstracted. There is an air of elaborate manners and ritualistic formality from another era. The characters move in and out of their roles with an obsessive, dance-like symmetry. Pauline Réage shows an extraordinary knowledge of fashion, and especially historical costume (we learn from *Confessions of O* by Régine Deforges (p. 28) that she once was a student of the history of costume). The clothes at Roissy are extremely theatrical; they suggest an eighteenth-century opulence, as in the paintings of Watteau and Fragonard. O is 'a captive in tawdry finery' (p. 11):

> a long dress with a full skirt, worn over a sturdy whalebone bodice gathered tightly at the waist, and over a stiffly starched linen petticoat. The low-cut neck scarcely concealed the breasts which, raised by the constricting bodice, were only lightly veiled by the network of lace. The petticoat was white, as was the lace, and the dress and the bodice were a sea-green satin. (pp. 14–15)

This is a courtesan's dress, which both constricts O and leaves her tantalizingly open.

When O first meets Sir Stephen, she is dressed entirely in black:

> black silk stockings, black gloves, her pleated fan-shaped skirt, a heavy-knit sweater with spangles or short jacket of faille. She decided on the jacket of faille. It was padded and quilted in large stitches, close fitting and hooked from neck to waist like the tight-fitting doublets that men used to wear in the sixteenth century. . . . The only bright foil were the large gold hooks like those on children's

snow boots which made a clicking sound as they were hooked or unhooked from their broad flat rings. (pp. 64–5)

O is progressively depersonalized by her fastidious costume. By becoming an art object, she also becomes a sex object – a living doll, whom men can use according to the way she titillates their fantasy.

In *The Image* too the clothing of Anne and Claire is always meticulously and exactly described. In Jean's dream vision in the final chapter, he sees Claire in her true splendor as a queen in a Renaissance painting:

Then I notice another woman in front of a brilliant stained glass window in an archway at the back. She is dressed in voluminous, sumptuous materials, like the Madonnas of the Renaissance. She is seated on a throne, her arms held out in a queenly gesture of welcome. She has Claire's face. She is smiling gently at me but with a far-off, enigmatic smile. (pp. 135–6)

A far-off, enigmatic smile like Leonardo's Mona Lisa? By archaizing the object of desire, by displacing it into another era with its own costumes and manners, the object gains brilliance. It is only in the present moment that it may be banal and unsatisfying.

It is a familiar paradox of both *Story of O* and *The Image* that, although the men are described as all-powerful, prepotent sexual beings, they nevertheless remain extremely vague. They may be deific forces hovering over the action, but they never assume their full identity as lovers and as human beings. Both books are almost entirely concerned with female sexuality, and the men are seen only through the women's eyes. It is essential for the sexual fable that the men remain in the background as undifferentiated and gigantic presences.

The whole relation between the sexes is bathed in religious imagery. Thus when O takes René's penis in her mouth at Roissy, she performs fellatio as if it were a consecrated eucharistic ritual:

O could hear the comments made by those present, but through their words she strained to hear her lover's moans, caressing him carefully, slowly, and with infinite respect, the way she knew pleased him. O felt that her mouth was beautiful, since her lover condescended to thrust himself into it, since he deigned to discharge in it. She received it as a god is received, she heard him cry out, heard the others laugh, and when she had received it she fell, her face against the floor. (p. 19)

René's ejaculation in O's mouth is described as a mystical experience, from the intensity of which O faints away. Like much of the sex in Sade, it is a public act performed in front of witnesses. In this way it is not private pleasure but ritual – and we may note how rigorously pleasure, or anything resembling personal satisfaction, is excluded from sexuality in *Story of O* and *The Image*. The sadomasochistic acts ensure the seriousness of the enactments, whose pain separates them definitively from mere hedonism.

O is consistently described in the religious terminology of martyrdom and sainthood. She is an ascetic who has voluntarily withdrawn from the world in order to deepen and fulfill her experience of love. Her soiled and defiled body is an instrument of some larger purpose. She sacrifices herself to some ideal of otherness. The whippings and the deprivations are tokens of some higher, transcendent reality which O is trying to achieve. She is purifying herself of selfish interests and worldly attachments. The persistent religious reference in *Story of O* underscores the paradoxical quality of this novel, which can be described as an erotic/religious fable in the style of Sade. The author delights in teasing the reader with religious and philosophical argument set in the midst of the most overtly sexual scenes. This is clearly in the tradition of Sade. In her long interview with Régine Deforges in *Confessions of O*, Pauline Réage confesses that 'I would have made an excellent nun' (p. 145), and she confirms the intensely religious coloring of *Story of O*. It is a novel of 'debauchery conceived of as a kind of ascetic experience' (p. 146).

It is O who deifies René and Sir Stephen, since we see them almost entirely through her eyes. To O, being in love is a religious experience described almost entirely in sexual/ theological terms. Her prostitution by her lover is a sign and portent that she is worthy to be prostituted:

> Thus he would possess her as a god possesses his creatures, whom he lays hold of in the guise of a monster or a bird, of an invisible spirit or a state of ecstasy. He did not wish to leave her. The more he surrendered her, the more he would hold her dear. The fact that he gave her was to him a proof, and ought to be one for her as well, that she belonged to him: one can only give what belongs to you. He gave her only to reclaim her immediately, to reclaim her enriched in his eyes, like some common object which had been used for some divine purpose and has thus been consecrated. (p. 32)

The vocabulary is specifically theological, and the author begins with a Christianized version of the amours of Jupiter, as in Yeats's poem, 'Leda and the Swan', and Giraudoux's play, *Amphitryon 38*. In order to become a consecrated object, O must give up her human qualities and her ordinary life in this world. This is one of the themes of the novel, culminating in the owl episode.

In some mysterious way, Sir Stephen is superior to René both as lover and as God. O comes to appreciate his love because it is so hard, so rigorous, so impersonal and so demanding – Sir Stephen is like the frightening and awesome God of the Old Testament, while René is closer to the God merely of love in the New Testament. René looks to Sir Stephen as the source of some special divine manifestation in O:

> All the mouths that had probed her mouth, all the hands that had seized her breasts and her belly, all the members that had been thrust into her and so perfectly provided the living proof that she was indeed prostituted, had at the same time provided the proof that she was worthy of

being prostituted and had, so to speak, sanctified her. But this, in René's eyes, was nothing compared to the proof Sir Stephen provided. Each time she emerged from his arms, René looked for the mark of a god upon her. (p. 106)

How is the 'mark of a god' indicated if not by some sign of beatitude? Our efforts to read *Story of O* as a dirty book are constantly being frustrated by its theological turn. And even sexually the book is remarkably distant in its purified and euphemistic descriptions of physical acts.

The Sade-like chateau of Roissy is represented as an educational institution or nunnery, where O is taught to forsake the world in order to be fully devoted to her lover/God. O moves toward what can only be described, inadequately, as spiritual illumination:

> Daily and, so to speak, ceremoniously soiled with saliva and sperm, she felt herself literally to be the repository of impurity, the sink mentioned in the Scriptures. And yet those parts of her body most constantly offended, having become less sensitive, at the same time seemed to her to have become more beautiful and, as it were, ennobled: her mouth closed upon anonymous members, the tips of her breasts constantly fondled by hands, and between her quartered thighs the twin, contiguous paths wantonly ploughed. That she should have been ennobled and gained in dignity through being prostituted was a source of surprise, and yet dignity was indeed the right term. She was illuminated by it, as though from within, and her bearing bespoke calm, while on her face could be detected the serenity and imperceptible smile that one surmises rather than actually sees in the eyes of hermits. (p. 44)

It is an extraordinarily bold move on the author's part to use religion as a vehicle of erotic fulfillment, yet there is a long Christian tradition of representing saints and martyrs in ecstatic union with God. We think of St Teresa (as in

Crashaw's poems) and St John of the Cross, and the author tells us in *Confessions of O* how much the scenes of torture were influenced by her reading in devotional literature (pp. 96–7). There is a constant ironic criss-crossing in *Story of O* of religious and sexual meanings. It is no mere idle gesture that Sir Stephen should nail up, opposite O's bed, a complete array of her instruments of torture: 'It was a handsome panoply, as harmonious as the wheel and spikes in the paintings of Saint Catherine the Martyr, as the nails and hammer, the crown of thorns, the spear and scourges portrayed in the paintings of the Crucifixion' (p. 166). It is in this spirit that O, in the hypothetical second ending of the book when Sir Stephen is about to leave her, asks his consent to die.

One side of the religious imagery of consecration/desecration stresses that O is guilty, that she believes herself wanton and that she considers herself justly punished for her sins. O is troubled by Sir Stephen's spontaneous insight that she is a sexual being in her own right:

> 'You are easy, O,' he said to her. 'You love René, but you're easy. Does René realize that you covet and long for all the men who desire you, that by sending you to Roissy or surrendering you to others he is providing you with a string of alibis to cover your easy virtue?'
> 'I love René,' O replied.
> 'You love René, but you desire me, among others,' Sir Stephen went on. (p. 84)

O's feeling of consecration is a way of atoning for her desecration, which she seeks both as a proof of guilt and a way of purifying it. She seeks the annihilation of a troublesome self that is too attached to the world. She seeks discipline and force to educate her, because she herself is ignorant and weak and without merit. When O imagines that René is losing interest in her and that she is no longer loved, she blames herself for not being worthy of him:

> She felt as though she were a statue of ashes – bitter,

useless, damned – like the salt statues of Gomorrah. For she was guilty. Those who love God, and by Him are abandoned in the dark of night, are guilty, *because* they are abandoned. They cast back into their memories, searching for their sins. (p. 92)

Who can be worthy enough for God? O feels the dark night of the soul because she is guilty and deserving of punishment, and the sin she keeps coming back to is her wantonness. This is sexual guilt, even though sexuality is also the path to enlightenment and beatitude. In a moving passage, O has a sudden childhood memory:

As a child, O had read a Biblical text in red letters on the white wall of a room in Wales where she had lived for two months, a text such as the Protestants often inscribe in their houses:

IT IS A FEARFUL THING TO FALL
INTO THE HANDS OF THE LIVING GOD

No, O told herself now, that isn't true. What is fearful is to be cast out of the hands of the living God. (p. 94)

O gives the Protestant apothegm a Catholic turn. She feels guilty and abandoned. She offers her pain as a redemption for her sins and a proof of love, but will God accept such a feeble offering? She is in a classic dilemma of religious introspection. It is both bizarre and exciting that she should seek redemption in her whippings, her prostitution and her whoredom. She is indeed being humbled, but, through love, she feels a mysterious connection with the godhead: 'Oh, let the miracle continue, let me still be touched by grace, René don't leave me!' (p. 94). She needs René, and later Sir Stephen, in order to feel that she is alive.

Story of O and *The Image* both depend on the idea that sex and love are a mystery, and both use surprising and unexpected transformations. At the end of *The Image*, when the initiation of Jean has been completed, the imperious Claire offers herself to him as his slave: 'I could beat her to death if it would amuse me' (p. 139). Claire can only repeat hypnotically that she loves Jean. All her other ingenious wiles have been sacrificed to, and have been preliminary to, this single truth. In Pauline Réage's preface to the *The Image*, she seems to be speaking for both books at once when she says that the reader must accept the sadomasochistic relation between the sexes as a mystery of enactment:

> Even chained, down on her knees, begging for mercy, it is the woman who is in command.
> She knows this only too well. Her power increases directly in proportion to her apparent self-abasement. But, with a single look, she can call a halt to everything, make it all crumble into dust. (p. 10)

Perhaps this preface explains why the all-powerful, sadistic men in *Story of O* are also so shadowy.

Pauline Réage takes the argument one step further when she asserts that women control the ritual in which they appear to be debased by men:

> Once this is clearly understood by both parties, at the cost of a mutual reappraisal, the game can go on. But its meaning will have changed: the all powerful slave, dragging herself along the ground at her master's heels, is now really the god. The man is only her priest, living in fear and trembling of her displeasure. His sole function is to perform the various ceremonies that center around the sacred object. If he falls from grace, everything is lost. (p. 10)

Thus Claire, no matter how submissive at the end of *The Image*, is still using Jean to fulfill her sexual destiny. Both Claire and O control the action because it is their book, and the men, although overtly dominant, only perform a priestly function in catering to the sacred object. It is strange to hear Pauline Réage making this overwhelmingly feminist and matriarchal claim for a sexual fable that is avowedly sadomasochistic. The man needs the woman as 'divine object', but the woman's 'only joy' lies not in the priest/worshiper man, but in the 'contemplation of herself' (p. 11). The man is only her instrumentality; apart from the woman, man has no autonomous function. As Pauline Réage tells Régine Deforges, 'in some surreptitious way, isn't she [O] in charge of them [René and Sir Stephen]? Doesn't she bend them to her will?' (p. 140).

O's passion to surrender her freedom is full of paradox. Freedom seems to mean not being attached, not being in relation to meaningful currents of sexual reality, being abandoned by God and your lover. It is an empty freedom. Being in love means surrendering your freedom to your lover. Of course O is always technically free to leave René and Sir Stephen and even Roissy (although Roissy is depicted in traditional prison imagery). O has of her own free will accepted her enslavement to René and Sir Stephen, just as they, for their part, have accepted their rigorous commitment to O. They are all actors who depend upon each other to complete their scenario. After O leaves Roissy, René labors a point that is already deeply understood by O:

> He began by saying that she should not think that she was now free. With one exception, and that was that she was free not to love him any longer, and to leave him immediately. But if she did love him, then she was in no wise free. She listened to him without saying a word, thinking how happy she was that he wanted to prove to himself – it mattered little how – that she belonged to him, and thinking too that he was more than a little naive not to realize that this proprietorship was beyond any proof. (p. 54)

In *The Image* too Claire is much more perceptive and sophisticated that the rather naive Jean, who has to be initiated into the sexual mysteries step by step.

O knows exactly what she is doing; to be a slave to your lover is a form of absolute commitment:

> She was no longer wearing either a collar or leather bracelets, and she was alone, her own sole spectator. And yet never had she felt herself more totally committed to a

will which was not her own, more totally a slave, and more content to be so. (p. 58)

The whole point of *Story of O* and *The Image* is that both O and Claire are in love, and they understand love to be a hard master. As in the Stoic doctrine, rigorousness is a proof of intensity. Both O and Claire are represented as being fulfilled and made happy by love. O has been branded by Sir Stephen and she wears rings on her labia 'proclaiming in bold letters that she was Sir Stephen's personal property' (p. 163), yet she has undergone the most extreme ordeals only as a proof of her profound devotion to her lover:

> The irons attached to the left lobe of her belly's cleft . . . came about a third of the way down her thigh and, at every step, swung back and forth between her legs like the clapper of a bell, the inscribed disk being heavier and longer than the ring to which it was attached. The marks made by the branding iron, about three inches in height and half that in width, had been burned into the flesh as though by a gouging tool, and were almost half an inch deep: the lightest stroke of the finger revealed them. From these irons and these marks, O derived a feeling of inordinate pride. (p. 163)

O has been set apart from other women. She has been chosen for special training at Roissy and special signs of distinction and grace. Although she considers herself a slave of love, she also thinks of herself as belonging to a small, highly select, sexual elite. As if in a dream where she has lost all power of volition, she is fulfilling her strange and ineluctable destiny.

The novel insists on O's free will. It is essential that her self-annihilation and quest for anonymity be a voluntary act. This is the central mystery of *Story of O* (and, in considerably less detail, *The Image*). In Roissy O moves toward a spiritual tranquillity that separates her desecrated body from her consecrated spirit:

> And yet nothing had been such a comfort to her as the

silence, unless it was the chains. The chains and the
silence, which should have bound her deep within herself, which should have smothered her, strangled her, on
the contrary freed her from herself.... Beneath the
gazes, beneath the hands, beneath the sexes that defiled
her, the whips that rent her, she lost herself in a delirious
absence from herself which restored her to love and,
perhaps, brought her to the edge of death. She was
anyone, anyone at all, any one of the girls, opened and
forced like her, girls whom she saw being opened and
forced. (p. 38–9)

The 'delirious absence from herself which restored her to
love' is the essence of spiritual conversion, in which the self,
with its petty needs, indulgence and pride, is annihilated in
some larger union.

O revels in her new-found sense of purpose and direction. Through the body, O has learned to be free of the
body:

She was no longer free? Yes! Thank God, she was no
longer free. But she was light, a nymph on clouds, a fish
in water, lost in happiness. Lost because these fine
strands of hair, these cables which René held, without
exception, in his hand, were the only network through
which the current of life any longer flowed in her. (p. 92)

What René represents as a person is left blank because it
does not really matter. René and Sir Stephen are in the
novel for the sake of O, and O is transformed by them and
by the power of love, whereas they remain exactly the same.
We are made to understand that any woman would satisfy
their impulses equally well. By the middle of the novel, René
has already transferred his allegiance to Jacqueline and Sir
Stephen is progressively abandoning O for other interests.
The men are shallow and promiscuous – not true devotees
as O is. The metaphysical and religious dimension in both
Story of O and *The Image* is reserved for the women.

In the course of the novel, O is opened, both literally and

figuratively, and this becomes a key word and concept. In what sense was she closed before? Closed to certain kinds of experience, especially sexual experience, that bring with them enlightenment. 'Open' and 'closed' are words for degrees of illumination. O cannot understand love until all her orifices are truly open. At Roissy her clothes open as she walks, exposing her sexual parts that are now available to anyone who wants to use them in whatever way. O can no longer hide herself. She is being deprived of any notion of privacy; she is open for anyone in the community. This is made explicit in the first speech of her masters:

> You will remember at all times – or as constantly as possible – that you have lost all right to privacy or concealment, and as a reminder of this fact, in our presence you will never close your lips completely, or cross your legs, or press your knees together. . . . This will serve as a constant reminder, to you as well as to us, that your mouth, your belly, and your backside are open to us. (p. 16)

O's first ordeal is to have her anus opened by an ingenious erotic device that she wears. When this procedure is completed, O is now 'doubly open' (p. 43) and will remain so. As in Sade, buggery is the preferred form of sexual union, perhaps because it demonstrates male insolence. It is usually represented as a solitary sadistic act, a rending by the man of a passive female.

O responds to the word 'open' in all its forms as if it were endowed with a magical reality: 'The word "open" and the expression "opening her legs" were, on her lover's lips, charged with such uneasiness and power that she could never hear them without experiencing a kind of internal prostration, a sacred submission, as though a god, and not he, had spoken to her' (p. 55). Thus 'open' becomes for O a sacred word, and it explains the meaning of her experience in the novel. 'She could not help thinking that the expression "open oneself to someone", which meant to give oneself, for her had only one meaning, a literal, physical, and in fact absolute meaning, for she was in fact opening every part of her body which was capable of being opened' (pp. 137–8). In an 'absolute meaning', the word and what it represents come together, so that there is no longer any distinction between language and the physical, psychological and ideational reality it represents. Pauline Réage is making demands on us to understand 'open' as a mystical word. After her experience with the branding and the rings, O 'would be returned to Sir Stephen more open, and more profoundly enslaved, than she had ever before thought was possible' (p. 153). Open and enslaved make for a difficult paradox, but to be completely accessible and available is also to remove all barriers between oneself and the world. This kind of enslavement is also the only true freedom.

'O' obviously stands for 'open', but the anonymous name, like a discreet character in an eighteenth-century novel, also has meanings. O is a conventional symbol of eternity, the snake with its tail in its mouth, which has neither beginning nor end. The O of the marriage ring symbolizes everlasting love, a circle that is lifted out of time and mortality. O is the hole, the cunt, female sexuality, which is either the eternal circle or an emptiness – zero – waiting to be filled. O is an exclamation of rapture, an emotive word for physical pleasure, as at orgasm. O is the tabula rasa, the empty white sheet of all women's experience on which Pauline Réage's novel is being written, since O only exists through the words of *Story of O*.

In the French title, *Histoire d'O*, there is a pun on 'O' and 'eau', or water, the feminine symbol of fertility, the fructifying element that gives life to all organic beings (the rain, the waters of seas and rivers, the amniotic fluid of the womb). O is the anonymous and pseudonymous heroine – 'that faceless, ageless, nameless (even first-nameless) girl', as Pauline Réage describes her in the preface to *Return to the Château* (p. 13) – and O's history or story or matter or affair (as we might translate the French 'histoire') is the life and adventures of Everywoman (an exact analogue of Everyman). It is not *The Story of O*, but the more abstract, impersonal and universalized *Story of O*. O is the depersonalized heroine, as Claire, when we first see her, is only a flat image or reflection of what she will become at the end of *The Image*: a reversed, mirror image of her transformation. *Story of O* and *The Image* are impenetrable mysteries that delight in sexual paradoxes, and especially in the towering paradoxes of slavery and freedom, the mind's attachment to the body, and the path that leads from whoredom to beatitude.

4 TWO SEXUAL LIVES, ENTREPRENEURIAL AND COMPULSIVE: *Fanny Hill* and *My Secret Life*

I T WOULD be hard to imagine two books more radically different than John Cleland's novel, *Memoirs of a Woman of Pleasure* (1749), popularly known as *Fanny Hill*, and the anonymous Victorian autobiography, *My Secret Life*, published privately in a few copies (and at the author's expense) in the early 1890s. Fanny Hill is an enterprising prostitute and madame, and her buoyant memoirs testify to a life well spent – colorful, varied, entertaining and lucrative. Walter, the somber, compulsive, self-doubting author of *My Secret Life*, is hardly a man of pleasure, although he has devoted his life and fortune to pursuing sexual experience, as much for his own education as for any hedonistic purpose. He seems trapped in two neurotic obsessions: to have an endlessly repetitive series of sexual encounters and to use them as the subject of his book, which is endlessly revised and perfected.

Fanny Hill is fiction; *My Secret Life* presents itself as non-fiction. *Fanny Hill* depicts joyous, pastoral, euphemistic sex, with dirty words and thoughts rigorously excluded; *My Secret Life* records an almost grim, daily round of sexual activity, mostly in urban settings, and with a remarkably accurate eye for physiological detail. *My Secret Life* is literally a dirty book because it is so filled with sexual juices that stain sheets and clothing, with the dangers of venereal disease, with piddling, with phimosis and with all the imaginable difficulties that impede sexual fulfillment. *Fanny Hill*, however, frees us from the anxieties attendant on pleasure.

Cleland's prostitutes are always nymph-like, well lubricated, good tempered and amazingly free of rashes, chafing, venereal diseases and pregnancy. They lovingly represent gratified desire in its commercial and consumerist aspect.

It is significant that the author of *My Secret Life* thinks so well of *Fanny Hill*. It is the only bawdy book that seems to him 'truthful' (p. 63), and he conceives his own book as a companion piece to it: 'Fanny Hill's was a woman's experience. Written perhaps by a woman, where was a man's written with equal truth?' (p. 63). But Walter, the protagonist of *My Secret Life*, objects to the stylistic restraint in *Fanny Hill*, which he will rectify in his own sexual history:

> That book has no bawdy word in it; but bawdy acts need the bawdy ejaculations; the erotic, full-flavored expressions, which even the chastest indulge in when lust, or love, is in its full tide of performance. So I determined to write my private life freely as to fact, and in the spirit of the lustful acts done by me, or witnessed; it is written therefore with absolute truth and without any regard whatever for what the world calls decency. Decency and voluptuousness in its fullest acceptance cannot exist together, one would kill the other. (p. 63)

So Walter will improve on *Fanny Hill* by making it even more truthful. It is odd that he thinks that *Fanny Hill* was written by a woman because it shows such fidelity to a woman's sexual experience. This is a tribute to Cleland's success in delineating Fanny Hill as his point of view character. It is her book and her life.

Fanny Hill plays an important role in the seduction of Jenny, a servant girl whom Walter visits, 'taking a pair of garters, two small showy neckerchiefs, and *Fanny Hill* with me' (p. 212). After Jenny prevents him from trying on the garters, Walter moves on to the book:

> 'Do you like reading?' 'Yes.' 'Pictures?' 'Yes.' 'I've a curious book here.' 'What is it?' I took the book out, *The Adventures of Fanny Hill*. 'Who was she?' 'A gay lady – it

tells how she – would you like to read it?' 'I should.' 'We
will read it together – but look at the pictures,' – this the
fourth or fifth time in my life I have tried this manoeuvre
with women. (p. 215)

Walter must obviously be using a well-worn copy of *Fanny
Hill*, as he flashes the bawdy illustrations that accompanied
the book in all early editions. Jenny protests: 'What a nasty
book – such books ought to be burnt,' but Walter counters
with sophisticated banter: 'I like them, they're so funny'
(p. 215). Walter intends to leave the book with her so that it
may work as a quiet aphrodisiac in his absence, but Jenny
threatens to burn it. The dialogue is wonderfully animated,
and the author has a fine ear for class distinctions in the
characters' speech. Although Walter eventually takes his
Fanny Hill with him (perhaps from fear that Jenny *will* burn
it), he does send it to her a few days later to prepare for the
next sexual assault. Jenny, of course, has *Fanny Hill*, open at
one of the pictures, on the very pillow of her unmade bed,
and after her seduction she sits in Walter's lap and they both
leaf through the pages together.

It is obvious that the author of *My Secret Life* believes in the
power of *Fanny Hill* as a sexual fiction able, along with other
suitable inducements, to move a woman to make love with
him. It is surprising that he doesn't think of *Fanny Hill* as so
radically different from his own book. In both, sex is central
– not only that, there is literally no other experience in the
books besides sexual experience. The world of these two
books is an entirely sexual place, and the other business and
concerns of life are quietly passed over. Sex is an entirely
natural impulse, so that it is not surprising to find the two
authors appealing to nature almost as frequently as does the
Marquis de Sade. Sex is an instinct that cannot be denied.
Once aroused, especially by a glimpse or touch of the sex
organs, the instinct presses for fulfillment regardless of
obstacles. The human will is no match against the forces of
nature, so that it is rare for the sex instinct to be diverted
once it is activated. Everything happens with magical swift-
ness and inevitability.

Fanny's early education as a whore depends strongly on understanding her own sexual instinct. When she has her first full view of an erect penis, she intuitively grasps the function of 'that wonderful machine',

> from which the instinct of nature, yet more than all I had heard of it, now strongly informed me I was to expect that supreme pleasure which she had placed in the meeting of those parts so admirably fitted for each other. (pp. 30–1)

This sounds like the sexual counterpart of the teleological argument from design, used in the eighteenth century as a proof for the existence of God. When Fanny and Louisa take possession of the idiot boy, a 'natural' in contemporary parlance, they find the vulgar saying – a fool's bauble is a lady's playfellow – amply proved: 'Nature, in short, had done so much for him in those parts, that she perhaps held herself acquitted in doing so little for his head' (p. 186). Fanny is an old-fashioned girl who finds any variation from heterosexual intercourse a violation of nature's simple plan for men and women. To Fanny, buggery is 'not only universally odious, but absurd, and impossible to gratify' (p. 180), and a homosexual scene she witnesses sends her into a tirade of righteous indignation.

My Secret Life interprets nature much more liberally, although Walter too is sickened with guilt at several of his own homosexual experiments. Both Walter and Fanny rely on nature to sanction their sexual impulses. They need to justify their lives given over to sex by an appeal to the freedom and honesty of natural instinct. Much of this is moralistic twaddle, especially on the part of Walter, who sees himself romantically in union with the great forces of the universe. He uses the idea of nature to mask his overpowering sexual compulsion, which drives him on almost without any sense of volition or choice. His philosophy of nature, simply stated, allows for all sexual acts that the human imagination naturally delights in:

> No blame attaches to woman for liking or for submitting

to such frolics, abnormal whims, and fancies, which fools call obscene, but which are natural and proper, and perhaps universally practised, and which concern only those who practise and profit by them. In my experience many women delight equally in them, when their imaginations are once evoked. Nothing can perhaps be justly called unnatural which nature prompts us to do. If others don't like them they are not natural to *them*, and no one should force them to act them. (p. 331)

In the repressive sexual climate of Victorian England, this is a bold and heterodox statement, whereas in the mid-eighteenth century when *Fanny Hill* was published, it would seem a more or less normal view of human sexuality. We remember that Fielding's Tom Jones is constantly betrayed into sexual transgressions from the warm-bloodedness of his nature. Everyone agrees that it is difficult to withstand nature's imperious force.

Walter celebrates the power of the imagination to extend simple copulation to more complex acts, which prove man's natural superiority to animals:

So are other erotic amusements equally natural and not more beastly. What more harm in a man's licking a woman's clitoris to give her pleasure, or of she sucking his cock for the same purpose, both taking pleasure in giving each other pleasure. So if a man plugs a woman's bum-hole with his finger when they are copulating or gamahuching [performing cunnilingus], and so with other sensual devices and fancies, they are all equally natural tho many may not enjoy them. All are permissible if a couple do them for mutual delight, *and are no more beastly than simple human copulation,* which is the charm of life – the whole object of life – and indulged in by all as much as their physical powers permit – yet it's not thought *beastly*. (p. 492)

Walter will not go down to posterity as a logical thinker, but he is trying passionately to believe in sex as the central mystery of human experience. His rationalizations are important to him in a way that contrasts with *Fanny Hill*, a delightful and frivolous book where reasoning and argument play almost no role at all.

Fanny Hill strives for an elegance, ease and insouciance that have nothing to do with the heroine's humble origins. It is in some sense a conduct book designed to show us the luxury and high tone that a successful whore can command, who mingles freely with the best society and who, by her natural wit and intelligence, is the darling of so many wealthy gentlemen. *Fanny Hill* assiduously cultivates the illusions of polite society: the dress, the manners, the style. Refinement and modesty are crucial to the theatrical effect. In Mrs Cole's brothel, for example, 'everything breath'd an air of decency, modesty and order':

> In the outer parlour, or rather shop, sat three young women, very demurely employ'd on millinery work, which was the cover of a traffic in more precious commodities; but three beautifuller creatures could hardly be seen. . . . Their dress too had the more design in it, the less it appeared to have, being in a taste of uniform correct neatness, and elegant simplicity. These were the girls that composed the small domestick flock, which my governess train'd up with surprising order and management. . . . Thus had she insensibly formed a little family of love, in which the members found so sensibly their account, in a rare alliance of pleasure with interest, and of a necessary outward decency with unbounded secret liberty. (p. 107)

The 'rare alliance of pleasure with interest' is like the society of John Gay's *Beggar's Opera* (1728), since it combines profit, or self-interest, with the material pleasures that money can buy. Fanny and Mrs Peachum would understand each other perfectly.

Mrs Cole's establishment is a stage set conjured up by the most blatant wish-fulfillment. Everything is easy and effortless on the part of both clients and whores, who act out their frolics with pastoral simplicity and the illusion of natural innocence:

As soon then as the evening began, and the show of a shop was shut, the academy open'd, the mask of mock-modesty was completely taken off, and all the girls deliver'd over to their respective calls of pleasure or interest with their men; and none of that sex was promiscuously admitted, but only such as Mrs. Cole was previously satisfied with their character and discretion. In short, this was the safest, politest, and, at the same time, the most thorough house of accommodation in town: every thing being conducted so that decency made no intrenchment upon the most libertine pleasures, in the practice of which too, the choice familiars of the house had found the secret so rare and difficult, of reconciling even all the refinements of taste and delicacy with the most gross and determinate gratifications of sensuality. (p. 109)

In typical fashion Cleland never goes into detail about any of these 'libertine pleasures' or 'gross and determinate gratifications of sensuality'. The book is constantly polite and well bred. It titillates without inflaming.

There is a secret life in both *Fanny Hill* and *My Secret Life*. Unlike the public and ritualized sex in Sade and his followers, these books insist that sex must be secret in order to be tantalizing, but Walter is obsessed and tormented by his secret life in a way that is unknown to Fanny Hill and her complaisant nymphs. He feels driven to seize reality and to control it by writing it down in his book. There is an abundance of physiological detail in *My Secret Life* that is entirely absent from *Fanny Hill*. It is important for Walter to touch and to feel all the sexual parts of all the 1200 or more women he has ever had, as if to assure himself of the reality of his own sexual existence:

I had from youth an excellent memory, but about sexual matters a wonderful one. Women were the pleasure of my life. I loved cunt, but also who had it; I liked the woman I fucked and not simply the cunt I fucked, and therein is a great difference. I recollect even now in a degree which astonishes me, the face, colour, stature, thighs, backside, and cunt, of well nigh every woman I ever had, who was not a mere casual, and even of some who were. The clothes they wore, the houses and rooms in which I had them, were before me mentally as I wrote, the way the bed and furniture were placed, the side of the room the windows were on, I remembered perfectly. (p. 64)

Everything is not merged into a single, homogenized sexual experience, but kept distinct and apart in all of its physical detail. This gives *My Secret Life* an extraordinary quality of sexual evocation.

The sexual detail in the book is not prettified, as it is in *Fanny Hill*, and it seems to be set down so exactly in order to refresh Walter's recollection. His past sexual life exists only in this book, and he doesn't want to lose any of the authentic details. His recollections of Mrs O*b***e, a lady from New Orleans, whom he meets in a Swiss hotel, are both vivid and disgusting. We learn, for example, that 'The hair in her armpits was thicker, I think, than in any woman I ever had' (p. 271), and this remarkable erotic discovery keeps re-appearing. 'Her head-hair was superb in its quality. I made her undo it, and spread it over the bed, and throw up her arms, and show her armpits when I fucked her' (p. 271).

Walter seems to revel in calling up the exact scene of his sexual encounter, with all its sordid by-products:

Our light burnt out, our games heated us more and more, the room got oppressive, I slipped off her chemise, our naked bodies entwined in all attitudes, and we fucked, and fucked, bathed in sweat, till the sweat and sperm wetted all over the sheet, and we slept. It was broad daylight when we awakened. I was lying sweating with her bum up against my belly, her hair was loose all over her, and the bed. Then we separated and she fled to her room, carrying her chemise with her.

Oh! Lord that sheet! – if ten people had fucked on it, it could not have been more soiled. We consulted how best to hide it from the chamber-maid. (pp. 269–70)

This is startlingly unlike most sexual writing, which strives for glamorous effects that ennoble the participants, who are always more or less engaged in heroic endeavors. Walter and the lady from New Orleans are strikingly unheroic. *My Secret Life* is remarkable for its depiction of the weariness, the soiling, the debilitating excess and ennui connected with sexuality. Yet Walter presses on to new conquests and new variations on the old experiences.

John Cleland delights in the poetry of sex, and *Fanny Hill* is a triumph of sexual rhetoric. Cleland self-consciously imitates the high style, with its flourishes of poetic diction and elaborate circumlocution. With deliberate amusement, he overturns decorum by elevating a low subject, but he asks the reader's indulgence for his figurative style:

> At the same time, allow me to place you here an excuse I am conscious of owing you, for having, perhaps, too much affected the figurative style; though surely, it can pass nowhere more allowably than in a subject which is so properly the province of poetry, nay, is poetry itself, pregnant with every flower of imagination and loving metaphors, even were not the natural expressions, for respects of fashion and sound, necessarily forbidden it. (p. 195)

Sex is a branch of the sublime, deserving 'every flower of imagination and loving metaphors'. In the eighteenth century the 'flowers of the imagination' meant rhetorical adornments. Fanny Hill strives for 'a mean temper'd with taste, between the revoltingness of gross, rank and vulgar expressions, and the ridicule of mincing metaphors and affected circumlocutions' (pp. 105–6), yet these apologies are obviously disingenuous. There are no 'gross, rank and vulgar expressions' at all in *Fanny Hill*. The novel steers much closer to 'mincing metaphors and affected circumlocutions', but the continuous good humor and satirical self-awareness remove any threat of a pretentious style. Fanny Hill is honesty itself, bluff, good-natured, and confiding in the reader as an old friend, confidant and potential or past client.

We take pleasure in the grandiloquent style of *Fanny Hill*, which perfectly expresses the prevailing sexual fantasies of the book. We are caught up in an imaginative world of sex as good, clean fun and not the tormenting obsession of *My Secret Life*. Cleland's physiological passages have little or nothing to do with human anatomy and neurology as we find it in Masters and Johnson and other medical and quasi-medical discussions. On the contrary, they are refreshingly abstract, emotive and imagistically evocative. The penis in *Fanny Hill* is much more a mechanistic and magical instrument than a recognizable organ of the human body. It is 'a column of the whitest ivory, beautifully streak'd with blue veins, and carrying, fully uncapt, a head of the liveliest vermilion: no horn could be stiffer; yet no velvet more smooth or delicious to the touch' (p. 55). The imagery is frankly hyperbolical, with the familiar oxymorons of Petrarchan sonneteering: the horn and the velvet are yoked with violence together. The effect is not to describe the penis at all, but to evoke the strongly contrasted, superlative emotions associated with sexuality. A column of the whitest ivory recalls the traditional love imagery of the *Song of Songs*: 'Thy neck is as a tower of ivory' (7:4).

Elsewhere Cleland celebrates the size of the male organ as a proof of enormous virility. Fanny's natural curiosity about the male sex suddenly reveals a very alarming mystery: 'playing, as it were, with his buttons, which were bursting ripe from the active force within, those of his waistband and fore-flap flew open at a touch, when out IT started' (p. 85). The penis is animated as a part of the body with an autonomous consciousness and energy. It has a life of its own unrelated, as it were, to the active volition of the person involved, and it offers a sexual display that does not seem to be connected in any way with its bearer: 'and now, disengag'd from the shirt, I saw, with wonder and surprise, what? not the play-thing of a boy, not the weapon of a man, but a maypole of so enormous a standard, that had proportions been observ'd, it must have belong'd to a young giant' (p. 85). But the owner is not a young giant at all, and Fanny can feel only the utmost surprise, mixed with awe and wonder:

> Its prodigious size made me shrink again; yet I could not, without pleasure, behold, and even ventur'd to feel, such a length, such a breadth of animated ivory! perfectly well turn'd and fashion'd, the proud stiffness of which distended its skin, whose smooth polish and velvet softness might vie with that of the most delicate of our sex, and whose exquisite whiteness was not a little set off by a sprout of black curling hair round the root, through the jetty sprigs of which the fair skin shew'd as in a fine evening you may have remark'd the clear light ether through the branchwork of distant trees over-topping the summit of a hill: then the broad and blueish-casted incarnate of the head, and blue serpentines of its veins, altogether compos'd the most striking assemblage of figure and colours in nature. In short, it stood an object of terror and delight. (p. 85)

Terror and delight were one of the mixed effects claimed for tragedy, and Cleland has already deployed a quasi-Homeric simile about the contrast between the black pubic hair and the white skin. This is all very fancy (if not fanciful), as Cleland wisely eschews any exact physiological description. The penis as 'animated ivory' is a frequent metaphor, which does not, of course, mean to invoke the extremely yellow and nicotine-stained appearance of authentic ivory. Cleland has a genius for aestheticizing sexuality, and Fanny Hill's encomiastic description of the penis transforms it into an eighteenth-century example of the sublime, vivid but highly idealized.

Orgasm is also extravagantly, pictorially and poetically represented in *Fanny Hill*. Its raptures are those of a soul in bliss, and any sexual reference at all disappears from the heightened emotionalizing. Euphemisms and circumlocutions are everywhere substituted for the vulgar and more prosaic actions of the human body, as in the following: 'we finished our trip to Cythera, and unloaded in the old haven'

(p. 195). Is Cleland thinking of Watteau's painting, *The Embarkation for Cythera*? Orgasm is 'the melting period' (p. 131), 'the sweet death' (p. 131), 'the melting swoon' (p. 163), 'the momentary extasy' (p. 142), 'a delicious delirium, a tremulous convulsive shudder, and the critical dying *Oh!*' (p. 189). It is 'the critical extasy, the melting flow, into which nature, spent with excess of pleasure, dissolves and dies away' (p. 31). Sex is a 'disorder too violent in nature to last long: the vessels, so stirr'd and intensely heated, soon boil'd over, and for the time put out the fire' (p. 56). There is a consistent sexual metaphor of fire and flow, and orgasm itself is an explosive dissolving and melting of the raptures that build up to the critical moment of release. This moment is often described in the familiar language of death and dying.

We can see Cleland's full panoply of rhetoric when Fanny Hill is reunited with her only true love, Charles, at the end of the book. His sexual union with Fanny has to make up for half a lifetime of absence: 'the sweetly soothing balmy titillation opened all the juices of joy on my side, which extatically in flow, help'd to allay the prurient glow, and drown'd our pleasure for a while' (p. 211). But this is only a temporary assuagement.

> Soon, however, to be on float again! For Charles, true to nature's laws, in one breath expiring and ejaculating, languish'd not long in the dissolving trance, but recovering spirit again, soon gave me to feel that the true-mettle springs of his instrument of pleasure were, by love, and perhaps by a long vacation, wound up too high to be let down by a single explosion: his stiffness still stood my friend. (p. 211)

The 'long vacation' is a bit of wishful thinking on Fanny's part, but one can see in this passage a typically mechanistic eighteenth-century view of sexuality: Charles's penis is an 'instrument of pleasure', whose stiff springs are highly wound and not to be unwound by a single burst. The image seems derived from contemporary horology; the striking clock can be depended on to strike again.

The sexual bout continues with renewed vigor, as Cleland's hyperbole grows grander and more grotesquely extravagant:

> Resuming then the action afresh, without dislodging, or giving me the trouble of parting from my sweet tenant, we play'd over again the same opera, with the same delightful harmony and concert: our ardours, like our love, knew no remission; and, all as the tide serv'd my lover, lavish of his stores, and pleasure milked, over-flowed me once more from the fulness of his oval reservoirs of the genial emulsion: whilst, on my side, a convulsing grasp, in the instant of my giving down the liquid contribution, render'd me sweetly subservient at once to the increase of his joy, and of its effusions: moving me so, as to make me exert all those springs of the compressive exsuction with which the sensitive mechanism of that part thirstily draws and drains the nipple of Love; with much such an instinctive eagerness and attachment, as, to compare great with less, kind nature engages infants at the breast by the pleasure they find in the motion of their little mouths and cheeks, to extract the milky stream prepar'd for their nourishment. (p. 211)

In this wild climax, Cleland gets lost in the 'nipple of Love' image, which seems to trace its origin to 'pleasure milked' and Fanny 'giving down' her 'liquid contribution'. Fanny's remarkable muscular powers of 'compressive exsuction' on Charles's penis (the 'nipple of Love') are compared to the infant at the breast, so that sperm is equated with the 'milky stream', and Fanny's athletic vagina works like those 'little mouths and cheeks' for Charles's ecstatic satisfaction. The literalness with which this bizarre image is worked out can only arouse mirth. It is certainly not meant to provoke a sexual response, since its roots lie in poetic diction rather than in any identifiable sexual reality.

The style of *Fanny Hill* is so different from that of *My Secret Life* that it is difficult to see how Walter could have fashioned his own book on *Fanny Hill*, which he believed was so truthful to a woman's sexual experience. *My Secret Life* is hardly a male sequel to *Fanny Hill*, yet Walter is hard pressed to find a suitable model for his sexual autobiography. In his neurotic need for affiliation, he seems to ignore completely both the poeticizing and the satirizing of *Fanny Hill*, which makes no pretensions at all to sexual sincerity. Cleland delights in teasing us with his mock-moral fable; *Fanny Hill* is frankly erotic in the best sense of that term. *My Secret Life* is not intended to be erotic at all. It is a literary monument to Walter's sexual life – in some important sense it *is* Walter's sexual life, since he must have spent more time in writing the book than in having the experiences on which the book is based. At times it looks as if he is having the experiences in order to write about them. Thus when he announces in his grand catalogue that he has never had sex with a Laplander (p. 618), we know that this egregious omission does not come about without effort on Walter's part, and that if a Laplander suddenly appeared, she would have an enormous sexual priority. Walter has a collector's instinct for the full series (with all the variations that specially appeal to collectors).

Walter is preoccupied with the truthfulness of his book, as if that could ever be verified. Ironically it is the truthfulness of the detail that contributes to the novelistic vitality of *My Secret Life*. He is not only describing his life, but evoking it. Walter kept rewriting and revising his *Secret Life*, as if the life behind it could in some way be perfected and made into a work of art. Everywhere there is a strong sense that history repeats itself and that life is a palimpsest. One woman recalls another in an endless chain, and one experience completes another, but the author seems to remain entirely static. Although he speaks constantly of his sexual development, at the end of the book he is the same voyeuristic, insatiable, guilty little boy that he was at the beginning. His book has not become the therapeutic instrument he postulated. It is only a monument to his satyriasis, his inability to be loved by any of the 1200 women with whom he has had intercourse, and his unlimited and monomaniacal capacity for disappointment and boredom. What if, at the end of his four thousand odd pages (in the unabridged edition), Walter should discover that one intense and completely satisfying orgasm in an entire lifetime was sexually superior to his 60,000 (calculated at the generous rate of 1000 orgasms a year for 60 years)?

Towards the end of his book, Walter sums up his experience of women with a little essay on how to distinguish the six major types of cunt: clean-cut, straight-cut with stripes, lipped with flappers, skinny-lipped, full-lipped and pouters. His discussion of pouters, for example, is entirely different in tone and spirit from anything we might find in *Fanny Hill*. It is not just physiological, but also full of alarming value judgments about what constitutes beauty and ugliness:

> The lips of these cunts are like half thin sausages, and almost seem to hang down from the belly, so that they leave a furrow between the outer sides of the lips and the inner sides of the thighs. It is the ugliest cunt – and is still uglier if the nymphae show much, as they often do. They look as if the owners were in a consumption. The hair on these cunts I have found often look straggling and thin – or if thickish, the bush is weak, long and with but little curl in it. Several times when I have found myself with a woman who had this ugly sort of genital, I have been unable to stroke her. (p. 624)

The last sentence is meant to arouse our sympathies for poor Walter, and the whole discourse is full of understood snobbery.

It is here that Walter unconsciously reveals himself and endows his secret life with Dickensian characterization:

> Pouters, like the thin lipped cunts – usually belong to women, lanky, thin, poor, ill fed and not too young, poor, short, skinny-arsed seamstresses, those whose bum bones you can feel. I fancy it is largely through want of

> nourishment in their case and frequently through ill health. Middle aged, needy whores – those who wear veils and try to pass themselves off as thirty when they are nearer fifty – have them. I have in my youth many a time been taken in by them, but never now go after a woman who wears a veil. (p. 624)

Like the many penises described in *Fanny Hill*, the pouter is given a life of its own apart from the woman to whom it belongs, although by synecdoche the veil is a sure sign of a pouter. The description is entirely characteristic in its animation and personification of sexual parts. It is pure sexual physiognomy, so that when Walter speaks of these six types of cunt, he is actually speaking about the six basic kinds of women. A mock-physiology has been substituted for psychology, and human character is sexualized in a way that narrows and reduces the possibilities of human motivation.

My Secret Life devotes one chapter to a plainly written sex manual suitable for adolescents. Walter wrote it while recuperating from a venereal disease, and it has a homely bluntness that is remarkable for its time. Sex is so vigorously demythologized and deromanticized that it becomes positively unattractive. The treatise begins with the most elementary propositions:

> Providence has made the continuation of the species depend on a process of a coupling the sexes, called fucking. It is performed by two organs. That of the male is familiarly and vulgarly called a *Prick*, that of the female a *Cunt*. Politely one is called a penis the other a pudenda. The prick, broadly speaking, is a long, fleshy, gristly pipe. The cunt a fleshy, warm, wet hole, or tube. The prick is at times and in a peculiar manner, thrust up the cunt, and discharges a thick fluid into it, and that is the operation called fucking. It is not a graceful operation – in fact it is not more elegant than pissing, or shitting, and is more ridiculous; but it is one giving the intensest pleasure to the parties operating together, and most people try to do as much of it as they can. (p. 355)

Cleland would have written this paragraph very differently, especially in trying to convey some notion of sexual pleasure through the heightened style. As it is, the pleasure is only postulated here, while we are treated to a whole series of negative disclaimers. If it is 'not a graceful operation' and 'not more elegant than pissing, or shitting', why do 'most people try to do as much of it as they can'? This must surely remain a puzzle to novices.

In contrast to *Fanny Hill, My Secret Life* avoids hyperbole and any of the flowers of rhetoric, but the sexual description is not literal either. Walter tries for a bluff, humorless, everyday style that will not glamorize sex. The result, however, is a kind of harshness and crudity that make sex seem like a necessary evil, as in the following description of sperm:

> Inside the body of the male are organs for secreting and forming a stuff called sperm, or spunk, which is whitish, partly thickish, and resembles paste which is thin and badly made, or thin lumpy gruel. This is spit up the woman's cunt, through the tip of the prick when fucking. This emission in popular language is called spending, or spunking, and is the period of the highest pleasure of the fuck, and the ending of it. This stuff is the male seed, and impregnates the woman, or as it is called in simple language, gets her in the family way. (p. 356)

Walter sees everything from the male point of view, and his language is consistently aggressive – sperm is 'spit up the woman's cunt'. The word 'spunking' does not well represent, phonetically, 'the highest pleasure of the fuck'. Walter's gruffness conveys a decidedly negative image of sexual ecstasy.

Walter is aware of the woman's pleasure, but so much of his sexual activity is with whores and servant girls that it is difficult for him to distinguish between sexual theatrics and sexual reality. All of his women are so randy, so wet and hot, and so unerringly swift in copious orgasms accompanied by moans, groans and passionate exclamations, that we are convinced that Walter is mistaking performance for fact. This undercuts his claims for unadorned, truthful depiction. For the reader, too, who sees all of reality through Walter's eyes, *My Secret Life* is subtly fictionalized. The book is not so much a record of Walter's sexual life as it is an image of Walter's desire. The author's inflamed fantasies shape the reality in which he moves, so that the distance between *Fanny Hill* and *My Secret Life* is narrowed. Why is Walter spending so much time writing this book if not, through the medium of art, to endow himself with an imaginative secret life entirely different from the not-so-secret life he is so avidly pursuing? It is clearly Walter who is the author of this life, and not the army of fecundating women who pass through its pages.

Fanny Hill makes no strenuous claims to truthfulness, yet her book reflects the social and economic realities of her time as deftly as Walter's more copious narrative. Fanny is left an orphan at the age of 15, and, like Sade's Justine at age 12, is forced to make her way in the world. She has no special training or skills. Her body is, in fact, the only commodity she possesses that has any marketable value, and a servant girl is virtually the only legitimate career open to her. The naive Fanny is quickly recruited into prostitution, where she learns so readily and is so sober and diligent that she is soon a kept woman and later a madame. Sade's *Justine* turns *Fanny Hill* inside out, because the one represents the triumph of vice and the other the failure of virtue. Justine keeps missing opportunities that the more resourceful Fanny capitalizes on to become wealthy. *Fanny Hill* is an economic success story that ends with the heroine reunited with her beloved Charles; her ample resources insure that they will live happily ever after. Fanny is a cunning entrepreneur, who, by the intensive, capitalistic cultivation of her own body, succeeds in a society whose values are entirely based on money. Like Defoe's Moll Flanders and Richardson's Pamela, Fanny knows how to exploit the limited resources available to her. She combines pleasure with profit and understands that virtue and vice are not moral absolutes but products of the 'force of conjunctures' (p. 77): 'But our virtues and our vices depend too much on our circumstances' (p. 71). Like a venture capitalist, Fanny puts her body out to use, by which she receives interest on her investment. At the end, Fanny is wiser and richer; she now can comfortably indulge herself in the sentimental effusions about virtue that fill the last few pages of the book.

My Secret Life turns importantly on money; Walter is distinctly upper middle class, and he can afford to buy the good things in life. Money plays a crucial role in this book, but often class is more powerful. It is common for Walter to seduce a servant girl, then offer money afterwards. His social position must have been irresistible to a servant girl, especially one in his own household. This is what is now called sexual harassment, although much more complex in its workings than its legal description would suggest. Walter always cuts a fine figure with simple girls of the lower classes, whom he dazzles with his sexual bravado. From his earliest youth he understands that servants are 'fair game' (p. 92). Walter is a gentleman, even compassionate, but he plays the game according to rules that favor him.

When he comforts the pregnant Lucy with strenuous intercourse, his mind is set idly to work on social distinctions:

> Her heavenly, voluptuous look as she spent I shall never forget. I was frantic with lust for her. Indeed had a love for her rapidly springing up; for not only did she seem to me, and indeed was the very perfection of sexual enjoyment, but was lady like in look, in voice, and in manner, and so utterly unlike a servant, that any gentleman, had he married her, might soon have made her a lady; yet here was this poor girl with child by a footman. As I laid by her side that day, I vowed to myself to do all I could to prevent her going to ruin. (p. 340–1)

It is Lucy's sexual genius that makes her seem so ladylike, but as much as Walter is moved by the ecstatic occasion, the thought never crosses his mind to marry her himself or to set her up as his mistress. There is a certain self-indulgence in his sentimental vow to help Lucy.

In another extended episode, Walter speaks of Sarah, the charwoman, who was hired to do the rough work in his household, but who is dismissed after coming home late from a sexual escapade. Sarah, who was a big, coarse, country girl before this, 'plain-faced, sleepy, and stupid-looking' (p. 244), suddenly becomes an object of sexual interest to Walter: 'I pitied the woman, but more than that from the time I heard that a man had assaulted her, a slightly lecherous feeling had come over me towards her. I wondered what he had done – had he felt her? – had he fucked her?' (p. 245). Walter begins to put his sexual fantasies into practice; he keeps touching her, talks dirty and gives her champagne, which she has never tasted before. He is both consoling her and seducing her at the same time, and in this confusion we feel the acute separation between master and servant. When Sarah is finally maneuvered into a house of accommodation, she is genuinely puzzled by her benefactor's determined sexual assault:

> 'You damned fool,' I said, 'I dare say fifty have fucked you, and you make a shame about your damned cunt, and your fears – what did you come here for?' She opened her eyes with astonishment at my temper. 'I didn't know I was coming here – I didn't know you meant me to do that – you said you'd be kind to me, and give me something to eat, sir – I'd not eaten since last night – you said you would be kind to me, sir.'
>
> It was said in the deferential tone of a servant. (pp. 252-3)

The dialogue is wonderfully poignant as we see all the assumptions of class and privilege set against a servant's tenacious fears.

We know that there is no way Sarah can possibly resist Walter's powerful arguments. What defence can a discarded servant girl make, who cannot get a letter of reference from her previous employer? Many eventually became prostitutes – 'went gay', in Victorian parlance. But Sarah continues to obstruct Walter's amorous cajolings:

> 'So I will, but if I'm kind, you must be kind to me – why should it be all on one side?' 'I'm sure I don't know,' she whimpered. 'You know he fucked you, and I dare say a dozen others have.' 'No one's ever done it but he, and he only did it twice,' said she blubbering. 'Let me.' 'No, I won't – I'm frightened to.' 'Go and be damned.' I put in my prick which had drooped, went into the adjoining room, put on my hat and coat, took up my stick, and returning to the bed-room, there was she still with her arse against the bed, crying. (p. 253)

Walter eventually has his way with her, as her resistance is broken down by harsh words, sexual caresses and frigging, and a tumbler of champagne. Sarah soon gets 'fuddled, not drunk, or frisky, or noisy, but dull, stupid, and obedient' (p. 255), and Walter enjoys his difficult triumph over her.

Why does he need these continuous triumphs? For Water, sexuality is a form of conquest. He must sally forth every day and do battle. Without obstacles there is no sexual pleasure. It is not just a question of money or of social class, although these facilitate his victories, but rather one of a certain kind of titillation. Walter is not ordinarily sadistic, despite his gross purchase of a nymphet to deflower, but he needs to use sex as a vehicle for proving his own mastery. We rarely hear of his relations with his peers; serving girls and prostitutes are better suited to enact roles that will flatter Walter. At the beginning of the book he is acutely conscious of his small penis, complicated by a painful phimosis which makes him fear that he will symbolically strangle himself to death. He is also worried that he will be interrupted during sex by his mother, and he in turn has his full share of primal scene anxieties. He is intensely voyeuristic, as if to assure himself of his own continuing sexuality, and although he indulges some of his homosexual fantasies, they also cause him intense feelings of guilt. Sexuality is both a burden and a pleasure to him. He is driven and he drives himself to copulate endlessly and to write about it endlessly. His secret life has a quality of solipsistic desperation about it. We feel a certain compassion for Walter because his secret life has so little to do with the secret lives of others, who remain casual actors in Walter's inflamed scenario.

5 SEXUALITY AND THE LIFE FORCE: *Lady Chatterley's Lover* and *Tropic of Cancer*

D. H. Lawrence and Henry Miller have more in common as novelists and as polemicists than may at first be apparent. Although radically different in style, both writers are prophets of a sexual apocalypse that represents a new freedom for modern man. Being in tune with your deepest sexual impulses also means being in tune with the life force. Sex is the manifestation of our intuitive, instinctive and primitive nature, which is vitally opposed to the constricting and stultifying life of the mind. In order to restore our wholeness and integrity, we must search out the power of the phallus and the 'phallic hunt' – in Lawrence's punning phrase (p. 231) – by which we assert our essence as human beings. By the fructifying power of sex – making love and babies – we are saved from a narrow and withering egotism that is the bane of modern civilized man. On these basic postulates, Lawrence and Miller would agree.

For most of his life Lawrence was under attack for being a dirty-minded writer (and painter too), so that *Lady Chatterley's Lover* in 1928 represents the culmination of Lawrence's earlier and less direct attempts at sexual themes. *Lady Chatterley's Lover* is very explicit sexually, and it also uses the familiar Anglo-Saxon dirty words without any attempt to euphemize them. In this novel Lawrence was taking a polemical stance and demonstrating to the world that he could write a frankly sexual book without any palliatives. It is not one of Lawrence's best novels, perhaps because it is so sexually programmatic, with Connie's sexual awakening worked out in an entirely predictable way. Despite Lawrence's deeply felt intentions for *Lady Chatterley's Lover*, sex becomes a mechanical force which is capable of working an almost magical transformation in the heroine. Her breasts, for example, are described on page 65 as 'rather small, and dropping pear-shaped. But they were unripe, a little bitter, without meaning hanging there.' By the time we reach page 206 they have become 'Her pointed keen animal breasts', which 'tipped and stirred as she moved'. This example is not significant in itself, but Lawrence wanted more for this book than it could possibly deliver.

When we read his impassioned defence, 'A propos of *Lady Chatterley's Lover*' (1929) in *Sex, Literature, and Censorship*, we understand that the novel could not hold all the deeply felt truths about sex that Lawrence wished it to contain. His almost mystical claims for 'blood-desire' and the mingling of bloods in intercourse seem to work against the novel's realization, where Connie and Mellors are highly characterized persons and not elemental representatives of the male and female principles.

Lawrence's profound convictions about sex are set forth in the essay on *Lady Chatterley's Lover*:

> The blood of man and the blood of woman are two eternally different streams, that can never be mingled. Even scientifically we know it. But therefore they are the two rivers that encircle the whole of life, and in marriage the circle is complete, and in sex the two rivers touch and renew one another, without ever commingling or confusing. We know it. The phallus is a column of blood that fills the valley of blood of a woman. The great river of male blood touches to its depths the great river of female blood – yet neither breaks its bounds. It is the deepest of all communions, as all the religions, in practice, know. And it is one of the greatest mysteries, in fact, the greatest, as almost every initiation shows, showing the supreme achievement of the mystic marriage. (p. 101)

The rapturous writing puts a terrible burden on Connie and

Mellors, so that their love-making, and especially their mutual orgasm, is made to bear a symbolic meaning that extends far beyond the physical pleasure. Connie and Mellors are intended to re-create the perfectly easy and natural persons, reveling in the joys of daily life, that Lawrence saw in the funeral paintings in Etruscan tombs (and described in *Etruscan Places*).

Henry Miller's theoretical stance about recovering the instinctual life is close to Lawrence, although very differently expressed. Sex is the life force in all of its manifestations, and Miller's commitment is to the body and to the intense flow of sensory experience. From this all else flows. Miller takes Walt Whitman as a kindred spirit, who was bursting with the joyous pressures of the sensual life. *Tropic of Cancer* is full of Whitmanesque poetry, especially the all-inclusive, vibrant catalogue of seemingly unrelated items:

> 'I love everything that flows,' said the great blind Milton of our times. I was thinking of him this morning when I awoke with a great bloody shout of joy: I was thinking of his rivers and trees and all that world of night which he is exploring. Yes, I said to myself, I too love everything that flows: rivers, sewers, lava, semen, blood, bile, words, sentences. I love the amniotic fluid when it spills out of the bag. I love the kidney with its painful gallstones its gravel and what-not; I love the urine that pours out scalding and the clap that runs endlessly; I love the words of hysterics and the sentences that flow on like dysentery. (p. 232)

This kind of writing is not amenable to logical analysis; it is itself a flow in the infinite regress of Heraclitus' dictum: 'Everything flows.' Like Whitman, Miller absorbs everything, negative and positive, into his Song of Himself, since the perceiving self of the poet is the only fixed point in all this random flow. Miller continues his universal panegyric:

> I love everything that flows, even the menstrual flow that carries away the seed unfecund. I love scripts that flow,

be they hieratic, esoteric, perverse, polymorph, or unilateral. I love everything that flows, everything that has time
in it and becoming, that brings us back to the beginning
where there is never end: the violence of the prophets,
the obscenity that is ecstasy, the wisdom of the fanatic, the
priest with his rubber litany, the foul words of the whore,
the spittle that floats away in the gutter, the milk of the
breast and the bitter honey that pours from the womb, all
that is fluid, melting, dissolute and dissolvent, all the pus
and dirt that in flowing is purified, that loses its sense of
origin, that makes the great circuit toward death and
dissolution. (pp. 232–3)

One of the flows Miller is celebrating is that of language
itself, and the words propagate themselves in a phonetic
rather than a logical sequence: 'hieratic, esoteric, perverse,
polymorph, or unilateral'. It is an abstract language separated from denotative meaning. To flow is to adopt a certain
permissive attitude to reality, and in this matrix of energies,
sex is one among many 'flows'.

Elsewhere Miller acknowledges his debt to Whitman as
the great poet of American life:

that one lone figure which America has produced in the
course of her brief life. In Whitman the whole American
scene comes to life, her past and her future, her birth and
her death. Whatever there is of value in America Whitman has expressed, and there is nothing more to be said.
The future belongs to the machine, to the robots. He was
the Poet of the Body and the Soul, Whitman. The first
and the last poet. He is almost undecipherable today, a
monument covered with rude hieroglyphs for which
there is no key. There is no equivalent in the languages of
Europe for the spirit which he immortalized. Europe is
saturated with art and her soil is full of dead bones and
her museums are bursting with plundered treasures, but
what Europe has never had is a free, healthy spirit, what
you might call a MAN. (pp. 216–17)

Whitman embodies the poet and the perceiver on whom Miller models himself. He is the great eye that sees all, the universal and sentient 'I' that feels all and experiences all. But Miller Whitmanizes only up to a certain point, when he steps back and laughs at himself: '*The body electric! The democratic soul! Flood tide!* Holy Mother of God, what does this crap mean?' (p. 241). Miller's saving grace is to be aware of his own inflated rhetoric.

Miller exploits feeling, and there is a continuous flow between the life of the streets and eating, drinking and sex. The body and its urges are part of everything else and not a separate, intellectual abstraction. 'The only life is in the streets,' says Miller in *Tropic of Capricorn* (1939), his acerbic autobiography of growing up in Brooklyn; and the first words of the first chapter of *Black Spring* (1936) are: 'What is not in the open street is false, derived, that is to say, *literature*.' The streets manifest living novels, so that the writer's primary function is to evoke memory. In *Tropic of Cancer*, on a Sunday morning, walking hungry in the streets of Paris, Miller sees the life around him in terms of his own needs:

> Hotels and food, and I'm walking about like a leper with crabs gnawing at my entrails. On Sunday mornings there's a fever in the streets. Nothing like it anywhere, except perhaps on the East Side, or down around Chatham Square. The Rue de l'Echaudé is seething. The streets twist and turn, at every angle a fresh hive of activity. Long queues of people with vegetables under their arms, turning in here and there with crisp, sparkling appetites. Nothing but food, food. Makes one delirious. (p. 35)

Miller is constantly projecting the astrological sign of the crab (Cancer) as his destructive symbol for the life of the city (and Paris is analogized to New York).

It is only one more step in the same continuum for Miller to sexualize the maelstrom of life in the streets, for sex is only another manifestation of this ceaseless activity. Thus the Square de Furstenberg is identified as a lesbian locale:

The other night when I passed by it was deserted, bleak, spectral. In the middle of the square four black trees that have not yet begun to blossom. Intellectual trees, nourished by the paving stones. Like T.S. Eliot's verse. Here, by God, if Marie Laurencin [a French painter] ever brought her Lesbians out into the open, would be the place for them to commune. *Très lesbienne ici*. Sterile, hybrid, dry as Boris' [Miller's roommate who has not invited him to lunch] heart. (p. 35)

Why are these four black trees described as 'Intellectual trees', and why are they like T.S. Eliot's verse and Marie Laurencin's lesbian playmates? Miller is making impressionistic links that cannot be scrutinized by cold logic.

The streets in *Tropic of Cancer* become mental constructs waiting to be converted into images by the perceiver. There is no question of an actual reality, but only of a reality that is projected by the all-encompassing mind of the writer/poet/rhapsode, who sees only what he wants to see:

On a Sunday afternoon, when the shutters are down and the proletariat possesses the street in a kind of dumb torpor, there are certain thoroughfares which remind one of nothing less than a big chancrous cock laid open longitudinally. And it is just these highways, the Rue St. Denis, for instance, or the Faubourg du Temple – which attract one irresistibly, much as in the old days, around Union Square or the upper reaches of the Bowery, one was drawn to the dime museums where in the show windows there were displayed wax reproductions of various organs of the body eaten away by syphilis and other venereal diseases. The city sprouts out like a huge organism diseased in every part, the beautiful thoroughfares only a little less repulsive because they have been drained of their pus. (pp. 36–7)

The logic of this passage is surrealistic. The diseased streets are seen in relation to the Tropic of Cancer theme: 'No matter where you go, no matter what you touch, there is cancer and syphilis. It is written in the sky; it flames and dances, like an evil portent. It has eaten into our souls and we are nothing but a dead thing like the moon' (p. 167). And therefore life is beautiful.

The whores that dominate the sexual life of *Tropic of Cancer* are another expression of the life of the streets. Sex is always easy and fortuitous, something a man happens upon during the course of a day – and sexuality is seen almost exclusively in male terms. The experience Miller is talking about is literally close to Walter's *My Secret Life*, yet Miller feels entirely different because he is so celebratory, so hedonistic, so high-spirited and, above all, so casual. Everything flows into and out of everything else, and there are no moral or social judgments. Next to Walter, Miller is a joyous innocent oblivious to the educational purpose of a life devoted to sex. Unlike Walter, Miller is never totting up his triumphs and entering them in his record book.

Thus the whore Germaine enters the author's life as a sexual hyperbole, with a single superlative quality:

> As she stood up to dry herself, still talking to me pleasantly, suddenly she dropped the towel and, advancing towards me leisurely, she commenced rubbing her pussy affectionately, stroking it with her two hands, caressing it, patting it, patting it. There was something about her eloquence at that moment and the way she thrust that rosebush under my nose which remains unforgettable; she spoke of it as if it were some extraneous object which she had acquired at great cost, an object whose value had increased with time and which now she prized above everything in the world. (p. 39)

Germaine's rosebush is a floral synecdoche for Germaine herself, who interests Miller only as a sexual being. None of the women in *Tropic of Cancer* are characterized beyond the few simple traits that make them attractive to men. They don't seem to have an independent being outside their sexual function.

Germaine represents the perfect sexual dualism: 'And

again that big bushy thing of hers worked its bloom and magic. It began to have an independent existence – for me too. There was Germaine and there was that rosebush of hers. I liked them separately and I liked them together (p. 40). We are more and more convinced that Germaine has been created out of Henry Miller's imagination. Not that she never really existed – only that her special magical quality has been fictionalized by the author. Miller is even half-aware of her theatricality: 'Most of the time she enjoyed it – or gave the illusion of enjoying it' (p. 41). But he insists on seeing her as a projection of male needs:

> But the principal thing was *a man*. A man! That was what she craved. A man with something between his legs that could tickle her, that could make her writhe in ecstasy, make her grab that bushy twat of hers with both hands and rub it joyfully, boastfully, proudly, with a sense of connection, a sense of life. That was the only place where she experienced any life – down there where she clutched herself with both hands. (p. 41)

This portrait avoids psychological detail. Germaine does not exist as a person in and for herself, but only as part of the phantasmagoria of Parisian street life and Miller's insatiable need for loving objects with which to people his private, imaginative world. Germaine derives her being only from Miller's autobiography.

The charm of it is that Miller has it both ways. He is rhapsodic, but he is also aware that he is being professionally entertained. He is tough and street-wise about sex and not to be taken in by appearances, no matter how flattering:

> When she lay there with her legs apart and moaning, even if she did moan that way for any and everybody, it was good, it was a proper show of feeling. She didn't stare up at the ceiling with a vacant look or count the bedbugs on the wallpaper; she kept her mind on her business, she talked about the things a man wants to hear when he's climbing over a woman. (p. 43)

So we never find out about the real Germaine, but only about the histrionic whore with the magical rosebush who has infatuated our author. It is not part of Miller's purpose to probe any further. He is content to take Germaine at her proven sexual value: 'she was ignorant and lusty, she put her heart and soul into her work. She was a whore all the way through – and that was her virtue!' (p. 43) There is no active misogyny in Miller, since he doesn't conceive of women apart from men. In the enormous narcissism of the poet, they exist for his pleasure. They are meant to prove the connection of sexuality with the life force.

Lawrence's style in no way resembles Henry Miller's, nor does the serious, ideologically committed, lean and consumptive Lawrence in any way resemble the Rabelaisian, bohemian, fun-loving and extravagant expatriate that Miller tried to be. To use a fashionable term, the two authors project very different personae, although Lawrence admired to excess the Dionysiac energies that we associate with Miller. It is as if Lawrence could only yearn to become his own physical and temperamental antitype. This endows his work with a certain heroic and romantic wish-fulfillment. The self-conscious humor of Miller is absent in Lawrence, although Miller can be deadly serious when he wants to be – the swollen 'philosophical' passages represent his writing at its worst. The one saving grace is that the worldly and sophisticated Miller is usually aware of his own pompous rhetoric and can suddenly break the mood. Unlike Miller, Lawrence shows us women at a certain distance; they are awesome and daunting objects. Yet Lawrence also has extraordinary sympathy for women, especially in their aspiration to find themselves emotionally and sexually and to unify the conflicting demands of the mind and the body.

When *Lady Chatterley's Lover* begins, Connie has already had a certain amount of sexual experience. With her young lover in Dresden she has given herself, but the 'sex business' was not attractive: 'The beautiful pure freedom of a woman was infinitely more wonderful than any sexual love. The only unfortunate thing was that men lagged so far behind women in the matter. They insisted on the sex thing like dogs' (p. 7). Connie yields to her lover in the 'sex thing', but she manages to preserve her sexual autonomy by an ingenious device known only to Lawrence:

> But a woman could yield to a man without yielding her inner, free self. That the poets and talkers about sex did not seem to have taken sufficiently into account. A woman could take a man without really giving herself away. Certainly she could take him without giving herself into his power. Rather she could use this sex thing to have power over him. For she only had to hold herself back in sexual intercourse, and let him finish and expend himself without herself coming to the crisis: and then she could prolong the connection and achieve her orgasm and her crisis while he was merely her tool. (p. 7)

Lawrence's sexual notions are alarmingly specific and physiological. The important point in this passage is that Connie holds back and doesn't give herself. She uses the man in order to have her own private orgasm, which Lawrence would regard as a form of masturbation.

We know how scornful Lawrence was of masturbation. In this area he was a thoroughgoing Victorian, with attitudes not much different from the dire warnings of William Acton (as set forth so vividly by Steven Marcus in *The Other Victorians*). In 'Pornography and obscenity' (1929), published in *Sex, Literature, and Censorship*, Lawrence inveighs against the 'merely exhaustive nature' of this secret vice:

> But in masturbation there is nothing but loss. There is no reciprocity. There is merely the spending away of a certain force, and no return. The body remains, in a sense, a corpse, after the act of self-abuse. There is no change, only deadening. There is what we call dead loss. (p. 73)

Masturbation is the direct product of pornography, which pervades our culture and undermines healthy sexuality. It negates the mutuality and reciprocity of two persons engaged in loving intercourse. It is a futile expression of a withering egotism:

> I think there is no boy or girl who masturbates without feeling a sense of shame, anger, and futility. Following the excitement comes the shame, anger, humiliation, and the sense of futility. This sense of futility and humiliation deepens as the years go on, into a suppressed rage, because of the impossibility of escape. . . . And this is, perhaps, the deepest and most dangerous cancer of our civilization. Instead of being a comparatively pure and harmless vice, masturbation is certainly the most dangerous sexual vice that a society can be afflicted with, in the long run. (p. 73)

How different in tone all of this is from Henry Miller, who would regard any expression of sexuality at all as a good thing. Lawrence's moral earnestness could only permit sex in certain prescribed channels, which he invested with a high ritual significance. To Lawrence, masturbation is a product of an urbanized, mechanized civilization destroying the life values, whereas mutual orgasm springs directly from the most profound and most natural sources of our being. Sex in Lawrence is deeply involved in dogma.

Connie's marriage to Clifford Chatterley, which is at the center of *Lady Chatterley's Lover*, is intimate in a friendly and social way – they are both articulate, refined and thoroughly upper-class persons – but it is never sexual. After a brief honeymoon, Clifford returns from the war physically shattered. When he recovers he is paralyzed from the waist down, and the 'sex thing' ceases entirely. Clifford, the lord of Wragby Hall and the director of the coal mines in Tevershall, symbolizes in a rather crude way the impotence of modern industrial civilization. His worldly position and power are inversely related to his sexual incompetence, whereas Mellors, the gamekeeper and a man of the people, is melancholy and disenfranchised but a super-stud.

Before Connie discovers Mellors, she has a brief affair with Michaelis (modeled on the writer, Michael Arlen), which once again leaves her deeply unsatisfied:

> He roused in the woman a wild sort of compassion and
> yearning, and a wild, craving physical desire. The physi-
> cal desire he did not satisfy in her; he had always come
> and finished so quickly, then shrinking down on her
> breast, and recovering somewhat his effrontery while she
> lay dazed, disappointed, lost.
>
> But then she soon learnt to hold him, to keep him there
> inside her when his crisis was over. And there he was
> generous and curiously potent; he stayed firm inside her,
> given to her, while she was active ... wildly, passionately
> active, coming to her own crisis. (p. 28)

Michaelis' passivity, albeit hard and erect, cannot satisfy
Connie's wild longings. She wants to lose herself, and especially her ever-present sophisticated consciousness of self, in
the wild abandon of orgasm.

She wants to recover a savageness and spontaneity that
has been lost to her. As a writer, Michaelis is a man of words
and the illusion those words create, rather than a powerful
and direct man of action. He only reinforces Connie's sense
of being trapped in an excessively civilized world of polite
gestures and talk. The very use of the word *crisis* for *orgasm* is
a sign of something seriously wrong with Connie's sexual
life.

Connie's deep depression over the loss of her erotic vitality reaches a low point in the scene at the beginning of
Chapter 7 where she examines her naked body in the mirror. Lawrence very skillfully endows this physical examina-
tion with the qualities of introspection, an externalization of
Connie's intense feelings of spiritual aridity. The dominant
imagery in this passage is from the vegetal world, and especially the image (and its negative) of ripening and coming to
fruition:

> Instead of ripening its firm, down-running curves, her
> body was flattening and going a little harsh. It was as
> if it had not had enough sun and warmth; it was a

little greyish and sapless. . . .

Her breasts were rather small, and dropping pear-shaped. But they were unripe, a little bitter, without meaning hanging there. And her belly had lost the fresh, round gleam it had had when she was young, in the days of her German boy, who really loved her physically. . . .

Her body was going meaningless, going dull and opaque, so much insignificant substance. (p. 65)

Without sexual fulfillment, Connie's body has lost its gleam. It is opaque rather than translucent, and Lawrence uses the Miltonic image of light for the illumination of the spirit. Connie hates the 'mental life', which has deprived her, by her own tacit consent, of 'healthy human sensuality, that warms the blood and freshens the whole being' (p. 66). She hates Clifford and all men of his sort who have defrauded her of her own body.

Connie's new body consciousness prepares her for her love affair with Mellors, her husband's gamekeeper. Clifford has already symbolically resigned his share in his wife by giving her permission to produce a baby discreetly with some other anonymous male. To Connie this relinquishment is the last tie holding them together. When Connie first makes love with Mellors, she is passive and dream-like: 'She lay still, in a kind of sleep, always in a kind of sleep. The activity, the orgasm was his, all his; she could strive for herself no more' (pp. 108–9). She knows that 'if she gave herself to the man, it was real. But if she kept herself for herself, it was nothing' (p. 109). So Connie holds back and wonders if, like O, she is easy and 'to be had for the taking' (p. 109). She is so numb and full of guilt that she cannot yet make love for herself, as an equal sharer. She has not yet awakened from her sexual/spiritual torpor.

In her next encounter with Mellors, she is beginning to feel stirrings of an overwhelming passion she hardly understands – a passion that frightens her. She perceives 'a new nakedness emerging. And she was half afraid. Half she wished he would not caress her so. He was encompassing her somehow. Yet she was waiting, waiting' (p. 117).

Connie is trying to come out of her separateness and isolation. She is trying to abandon her position as mental observer of her own sensual life. She keeps apart and makes withering observations. Thus the thrusting of the man's buttocks seems 'supremely ridiculous' to her because she is a passive recipient whose consciousness has not been unified by sexual union. Connie's psychological development runs an exact parallel to her sexual development.

When she finally reaches climactic orgasm with Mellors, Lawrence is at a loss for words that can adequately represent what Connie feels. It is a great breakthrough, yet all she can do is to parody lines from Romantic poetry (especially Poe and Byron) with the familiar imagery of the ebb and flow of the sea, of flames, of music. There is a certain mindless exuberance in all this that doesn't come naturally to Lawrence:

> Then as he began to move, in the sudden helpless orgasm, there awoke in her new strange trills rippling inside her. Rippling, rippling, rippling, like a flapping overlapping of soft flames, soft as feathers, running to points of brilliance, exquisite, exquisite and melting her all molten inside. It was like bells rippling up and up to a culmination. She lay unconscious of the wild little cries she uttered at the last. (pp. 124–5)

The tinkling jingles of Poe's 'Bells' are reincarnated in orgasm, as Connie feels the power of something outside her volition.

She has finally been able to cast off the burden of her modern self-consciousness:

> She clung to him unconscious in passion, and he never quite slipped from her, and she felt the soft bud of him within her stirring, and strange rhythms flushing up into her with a strange rhythmic growing motion, swelling and swelling till it filled all her cleaving consciousness, till she was one perfect concentric fluid of feeling, and she

lay there crying in unconscious inarticulate cries. The voice out of the uttermost night, the life! (p. 125)

Her 'unconscious inarticulate cries' are part of a deeper and more primitive being, like the sea, and one of Lawrence's most powerful images is that of Connie 'softly clamouring, like a sea-anemone under the tide' (p. 125). Otherwise, the passage has an onomatopoetic quality that tries to imitate the sounds and rhythms of orgasm without describing it directly. The emotional evocation is strong but obvious, and one might object that Lawrence has overwritten his emotional climax. It was grand but not persuasive.

Connie now experiences a conflict between her adoration of Mellors the man, and father of her newly conceived child, and her contempt for Mellors as the impersonal, phallic instrument which assuages her bacchic frenzy. Lawrence recreates the orgiastic rites of the mystery religions of ancient Greece:

> Ah yes, to be passionate like a Bacchante, like a Bacchanal fleeing through the woods, to call on Iacchos, the bright phallos that had no independent personality behind it, but was pure god-servant to the woman! The man, the individual, let him not dare intrude. He was but a temple-servant, the bearer and keeper of the bright phallos, her own.
>
> So, in the flux of new awakening, the old hard passion flamed in her for a time, and the man dwindled to a contemptible object, the mere phallos-bearer, to be torn to pieces when his service was performed. She felt the force of the Bacchae in her limbs and her body, the woman gleaming and rapid, beating down the male. (p. 127)

This passage has a matriarchal ring to it, but Connie wants to 'give up her hard bright female power' in order to 'sink in the new bath of life' (p. 127). Her surrender is one of adoration, because she is convinced that her barrenness has ended and that Mellors has quickened her with new life. The whole scene is bathed in a quasi-religious glow as sexuality fulfills a higher purpose. Lawrence had great temperamental difficulties in writing about pure pleasure and ecstasy, a problem Miller never had to cope with, so that Lawrence's descriptions of orgasm have the rhetorical artificiality of *Fanny Hill* without the cheerful exuberance.

When Connie and Mellors run naked in the rain, it is as if they have become pagan fertility gods. Mellors takes her on the ground, 'short and sharp ... like an animal' (p. 207), which is right for the symbolism of the novel, where sex is restored to blood lust and primitive rituals. It is crucial for Lawrence to banish sex in the mind and the narcissistic, self-regarding and titillating sex of an urban, mechanistic civilization. When Connie and Mellors decorate their naked bodies with wild flowers, they seem to be completing a religious ritual, where the nature gods must be appropriately decorated for the occasion. It is the pastoral innocence of Perdita and Florizel in the sheep-shearing scene of Shakespeare's *Winter's Tale* realized in all of its erotic implications.

Mellors celebrates Connie's body in his Derbyshire dialect:

> 'Tha'rt real, tha art! Tha'rt real, even a bit of a bitch. Here tha shits an' here tha pisses: an' I lay my hand on 'em both an' like thee for it. I like thee for it. Tha's got a proper, woman's arse, proud of itself. It's none ashamed of itself, this isna.'
>
> He laid his hand close and firm over her secret places, in a kind of close greeting. (p. 208)

It's surprising to find Lawrence using sexual euphemisms worthy of *Fanny Hill* at this climactically frank moment. 'Secret places' sounds very Victorian, as does the much repeated phrase 'secret skin'. And Mellors' dialect has a comically theatrical cast to it; it is not so much earthy as cute. But the dialect asserts a physical and geographical reality that undercuts any excessively heightened feeling of mythological re-enactment.

The erotic high point of *Lady Chatterley's Lover* is Connie's 'night of sensual passion' (p. 231) before she separates temporarily from Mellors toward the end of the novel. There is an unfortunate vagueness about what happens to Connie on this memorable night, but the passage is usually interpreted to imply, among other things, anal intercourse, since Mellors is rumored to have used his wife, 'as Benvenuto Cellini says, "in the Italian way" ' (p. 250). Whatever actually occurs, Connie experiences a frightening and profound sensuality she has never known before:

> It was a night of sensual passion, in which she was a little startled and almost unwilling: yet pierced again with piercing thrills of sensuality, different, sharper, more terrible than the thrills of tenderness, but, at the moment, more desirable. Though a little frightened, she let him have his way, and the reckless, shameless sensuality shook her to her foundations, stripped her to the very last, and made a different woman of her. It was not really love. It was not voluptuousness. It was sensuality sharp and searing as fire, burning the soul to tinder. (p. 231)

This passage represents Lawrence's sexual writing at its worst, since the 'phallic hunting out' Connie undergoes in order to emerge 'naked and unashamed' (p. 232) is more a matter of inflated rhetoric than experience that can be painfully felt. The passage is not only overwritten, it is also prissy, as Connie reluctantly accedes to Mellors' lower-class and street-wise sexual demands. Connie's 'night of sensual passion' is a kind of slumming, and it is clear that it can only happen once.

Connie abundantly resembles O in her sexual transformation, but O never glorifies or romanticizes her willing degradation. Her pain and her torment are always paradoxical, whereas Connie's is too openly celebratory. She is so proud of her accomplishment – she a middle-class woman, mistress of Wragby Hall – that we feel a certain smugness in her stoic endurance:

Burning out the shames, the deepest, oldest shames, in the most secret places. It cost her an effort to let him have his way and his will of her. She had to be a passive, consenting thing, like a slave, a physical slave. Yet the passion licked round her, consuming, and when the sensual flame of it pressed through her bowels and breast, she really thought she was dying: yet a poignant, marvellous death.

She had often wondered what Abélard meant, when he said that in their year of love he and Héloïse had passed through all the stages and refinements of passion. The same thing, a thousand years ago: ten thousand years ago! The same on the Greek vases, everywhere! The refinements of passion, the extravagances of sensuality! And necessary, forever necessary, to burn out false shames and smelt out the heaviest ore of the body into purity. With the fire of sheer sensuality. (p. 231)

While the reader is hungering for some honest, lurid details, Lawrence is launching inflamed exclamations of historical continuity. Lawrence's sexual imagination fails him at this point, and Connie is forced to undergo what can only be understood as an implied experience.

If sex is indeed the life force, it is a pleasure to turn from Lawrence's high-flown declarations of purpose to Miller's vulgar but equally exuberant celebrations of cunt. Miller is not subtle, but an enthusiast. He passes his words around as if they were the best champagne, to be imbibed directly from the bottle in maudlin camaraderie. His celebration of Tania in *Tropic of Cancer* is extravagant and irresponsible – it is ultimately a celebration of himself – yet there is an easy joyousness in it that eluded Lawrence. Connie is much more convincing in her opaque adversity than in her trilling orgasms and her searingly phallic night of sensual passion. Tania, on the other hand, is a grandiose, Russian-Jewish princess who exists only as a figment of Miller's overheated sexual hyperboles:

O Tania, where now is that warm cunt of yours, those fat,

heavy garters, those soft, bulging thighs? There is a bone in my prick six inches long. I will ream out every wrinkle in your cunt, Tania, big with seed. I will send you home to your Sylvester with an ache in your belly and your womb turned inside out. Your Sylvester! Yes, he knows how to build a fire, but I know how to inflame a cunt. I shoot hot bolts into you, Tania, I make your ovaries incandescent. Your Sylvester is a little jealous now? He feels something, does he? He feels the remnants of my big prick. (p. 5)

This is all mock-heroic, pure Whitman, but Whitman as clown, sage and Priapus all in one. Miller is teasing us with his sexual cadenza. It is a performance for its own sake, and the sheer fun of it is radically different from anything in Lawrence.

In his adulatory essay, 'Henry Miller: genius and lust, narcissism', Norman Mailer shrewdly observes that Miller is not a social writer like Lawrence, but one of our few sexual writers:

Even Lawrence never let go of the idea that through sex he could still delineate society; Miller, however, went further. Sex, he assumed, was a natural literary field for the novel, as clear and free and open to a land-grab as any social panorama. One could capture the sex-life of two people in all its profundity and have quite as much to say about the cosmos as any literary plot laid out the other way with its bankers and beggars, ladies and whores, clerks and killers. The real novel, went Miller's assumption, could short-circuit society. Give us the cosmos head on. Give it to us by way of a cunt impaled on a cock. (p. 33)

It is obviously Miller's example and not Lawrence's that lies behind Mailer's attempts to be a sexual writer in *An American Dream* (1965). The attempt fails because the sexual reality is not large enough to serve as metonymy for the social reality. Unlike Henry Miller's bold hyperboles, the heavily symbolic sexual reality in *An American Dream* does not convincingly 'Give us the cosmos head on'.

Miller's irreverence complements Lawrence's gravity. Connie is awakened to a new sense of life around her. Her body comes alive and she understands that all truth must be perceived through the senses. Her discovery of sex is an illumination, but once she has been enlightened it seems as if she doesn't know what to do with her new knowledge. She is naked and unashamed, but Mellors is still the same as ever, and it is difficult to see why Lawrence used such a blank, narrow and ungenerous male protagonist. Like René and Sir Stephen in *Story of O*, Mellors remains a shadowy presence representing the male principle, while O and Connie dominate the experience of both books.

Miller's *Tropic of Cancer* is distinctly a male book – Miller didn't know how to write any other kind. The autobiographical 'I' controls the action. Despite extravagance and surrealistic fantasy, it is Miller's life that is novelistically rendered without the burden of objectification and the division of a single, multifarious subject into separate consciousnesses. We get to know the 'I' of the book and we appreciate his continuity. We sympathize with him in his rhapsodic confrontation of all experience; his book, after all, is a sexual epic and he is its eponymous hero:

> I have no money, no resources, no hopes. I am the happiest man alive. A year ago, six months ago, I thought that I was an artist. I no longer think about it, I *am*. Everything that was literature has fallen from me. There are no more books to be written, thank God. (p. 1)

This is, of course, the prolegomenon to *Tropic of Cancer*, from which all else follows. Lawrence is circumstantial and philosophical and moral where Miller is only declarative. What could be more artful and all-inclusive than to assert simply: 'I *am*'?

6 SEXUALITY AND SELF-FULFILLMENT: *Portnoy's Complaint* and *Fear of Flying*

E RICA JONG's *Fear of Flying* (1973) is conceived on the model of Philip Roth's *Portnoy's Complaint* (1969). Although the two novels are radically different in many respects, Portnoy and Isadora seem mirror images of each other, especially in their search for the good life. Why this search must be conducted in terms of sex is one of the recurrent mysteries of sexual fiction. Both novels are drenched in sexuality, sometimes raw, crude and disgusting, but always earthy and significant. Both novels feel powerfully autobiographical and sincere, and if sincere, therefore authentic.

The sexual choices are steeped in moral significance, but they are genuinely sexual nevertheless. Good Sex becomes the big equivalent of the Good Life, and the demands of the id are urgently flashed on the screen of consciousness. 'LET'S PUT THE ID BACK IN YID!' shouts Portnoy to his psychoanalyst. 'Liberate this nice Jewish boy's libido, will you please? Raise the prices if you have to – I'll pay anything! Only enough cowering in the face of the deep, dark pleasures!' (pp. 124–5) Those romantically deep and dark pleasures are constantly eluding the troubled Portnoy, and they always seem just out of reach for the tantalized Isadora, who cannot solve the basic paradox of being a woman: 'I was furious with my mother for not teaching me how to be a woman, for not teaching me how to make peace between the raging hunger in my cunt and the hunger in my head' (p. 154).

Both novels are comic in spirit, but neither is happy. Portnoy and Isadora go through a series of adventures or misadventures – almost a sexual picaresque – that are not only not satisfying, but also frustrating, demeaning and more than a little masochistic. They are, in their own ways, pathetic antiheroes of their own inflamed imaginations. Sex is the Holy Grail that drives them on in a quest that is doomed to failure. Neither Portnoy nor Isadora ever properly matures into an adult, but remains fixated in adolescent longings that can never be satisfied. Although Portnoy is 33 and Isadora 29, they seem much younger. Their stories are recollections of an unfulfilled youth – or perhaps an attempt to relive these formative years more successfully. Portnoy uses psychoanalysis to repair his life, and although psychoanalysis is crucial in *Fear of Flying*, Isadora tries to find herself (and recover her identity) through being a writer.

Everywhere in the two novels the demands of the mind and the body are set against each other in a rigid and irreconcilable dualism. Perhaps sexual fiction, by its insistence on physical pleasure, is almost necessarily committed to this dualism. It is certainly at the heart of Sade's works, whose characters alternate regularly between orgies and philosophical discussions. Without the intellect, there would be no way to understand and appreciate erotic experience, but without the intellect there would also be no sadness and disappointment at 'Th' expense of spirit in a waste of shame' (Shakespeare, Sonnet 129).

Behind *Portnoy's Complaint* lies psychoanalysis, and especially Freud's essay, 'The most prevalent form of degradation in erotic life' (1912). This is one of the chapter headings in Roth's novel, and Portnoy tells us how much he is under the influence of this essay, because it seems to explain his preoccupation with *shikses* (non-Jewish girls): 'Is it true that only if the sexual object fulfills for me the condition of being degraded, that sensual feeling can have free play?' (p. 186) Portnoy is thinking of his infatuation with the Monkey, 'a nickname that derives from a little perversion she once engaged in shortly before meeting me and going on to grander things' (p. 106). The Monkey is a sexual being, almost illiterate, who fulfills Portnoy's sexual velleities but whom he cannot love because, in Freud's explanation, she conflicts with his incestuous attachment to his mother.

Portnoy suffers from the classic conflict between woman as mother/madonna and woman as whore. In order to be able to enjoy sex at all, he must degrade his object-choice so that she is as unlike his mother as possible. In this he is only partly successful, since Portnoy's Complaint expresses itself, according to Dr O. Spielvogel, in 'Acts of exhibitionism, voyeurism, fetishism, auto-eroticism and oral coitus', and 'neither fantasy nor act issues in genuine sexual gratification, but rather in overriding feelings of shame and the dread of retribution, particularly in the form of castration'. In other words, for Portnoy sex has to be dirty in order to be good. Sexual acts, however, are by their very finiteness totally inadequate to satisfy Portnoy's obsessive imagination. His satyriasis is steeped in incestuous guilt – his frenzied efforts to defy Mrs Portnoy are self-defeating – and sex never brings the Technicolor rewards it promises.

Freud's essay is crucial for understanding *Portnoy's Complaint* and much else in sexual fiction. Basically, Freud sees a conflict between the primitive, animal urges of sexuality and the demands of culture and civilization. It is 'not possible for the claims of the sexual instinct to be reconciled with the demands of culture' (p. 186), and 'something in the nature of the sexual instinct itself is unfavourable to the achievement of absolute gratification' (p. 184). If there are two currents of feeling necessary for 'a fully normal attitude in love' – 'the tender, affectionate feelings and the sensual feelings' – then it is extraordinarily difficult to bring these two currents together (p. 174). This is the cause of impotence in men and perhaps of frigidity in women, that sex is base and degrading and cannot be reconciled with love. An incestuous attachment to the mother (or sister) blocks the release of sensual feelings toward the love object, which must be degraded in order to be sexual. In other words, the incestuous feelings of tenderness and affection must be

exorcised in order for the lover to experience sexual fulfillment. The love-object must therefore be as unlike the
mother (or sister) as possible in order to free the male from
disabling incestuous guilt. The problem is to overcome a
dissociative erotic sensibility: 'Where such men love they
have no desire and where they desire they cannot love. In
order to keep their sensuality out of contact with the objects
they love, they seek out objects whom they need not love'
(p. 177). 'As soon as the sexual object fulfils the condition of
being degraded, sensual feeling can have free play' (p. 178).

Freud was genuinely concerned with problems of impotence and frigidity, which he saw as one of the leading
symptoms of neurosis. These problems are closely intertwined with civilization and its discontents. The kind of
high-minded, middle-class women available to a man of
standing and culture are not those designed to satisfy his
sexual longings, so that the two currents of feeling needed
for 'a fully normal attitude in love' are hopelessly in conflict
with each other. There is a certain wistful regret in Freud's
depiction of this sexual schism:

> In only very few people of culture are the two strains of
> tenderness and sensuality duly fused into one; the man
> almost always feels his sexual activity hampered by his
> respect for the woman and only develops full sexual
> potency when he finds himself in the presence of a lower
> type of sexual object; and this again is partly conditioned
> by the circumstance that his sexual aims include those of
> perverse sexual components, which he does not like to
> gratify with a woman he respects. Full sexual satisfaction
> only comes when he can give himself up wholeheartedly
> to enjoyment, which with his well-brought-up wife, for
> instance, he does not venture to do. Hence comes his
> need for a less exalted sexual object, a woman ethically
> inferior, who does not know the rest of his life and cannot
> criticize him. It is to such a woman that he prefers to
> devote his sexual potency, even when all the tenderness
> in him belongs to one of a higher type. (p. 180)

Fear of incest is, therefore, not the only blocking factor in sexual expression; our civilization, with its hierarchy of values, status and social refinement, also inhibits the free play of sexual urges. With great daring (and much hesitation as well), Freud enunciates a heterodox principle: 'It has an ugly sound and a paradoxical as well, but nevertheless it must be said that whoever is to be really free and happy in love must have overcome his deference for women and come to terms with the idea of incest with mother or sister' (p. 181). But 'to be really free and happy in love' is not one of Freud's highest ideals. He seems to prefer the sublimation of sensuality in demanding, creative work.

Freud tentatively extends his essay to women, and especially to problems of frigidity, by postulating a female equivalent to the male need to degrade the sexual object:

> In my opinion the necessary condition of forbiddenness in the erotic life of women holds the same place as the man's need to lower his sexual object. Both are the consequence of the long period of delay between sexual maturity and sexual activity which is demanded by education for social reasons. (p. 182)

In other words, women cultivate secrecy and intrigue in order to stimulate their sensuality; what is open and permissible loses its spice. This theory may be demonstrated from the melodramatic fantasies of *My Secret Garden*, but in *Fear of Flying* too the guilty scenarios help to fuel a sense of forbidden (and therefore gratifying) sex. The lover is, by definition, more attractive than the husband, and difficult love is more exciting than love that is easily attained and comfortably consummated. Isadora's poetic imagination is fed by secret trysts and the satisfaction of spontaneous/compulsive desires in the face of a disapproving world. As a sexual being she defies the law and order of marriage, monogamy and what is expected from a good Jewish girl – in other words, she defies not only the mores of western civilization, but also, and perhaps more importantly, those of the Upper West Side of Manhattan. Isadora is never far from acting out her mother's first piece of advice: 'Above all, never be *ordinary*' (p. 147). She avoids the ordinary with all the histrionic means at her disposal.

In *Portnoy's Complaint* Mrs Portnoy represents all of the forbidding social values Alex is rebelling against. Her impossibly high standards of cleanliness, personal hygiene, nutrition and achievement in life are a parody of the American Way of Life as seen from the perspective of the Jewish ghetto in Newark, New Jersey. Sophie Portnoy wants only the best for her son – to be a good boy and a little gentleman – but Alex is suffering from an overdeveloped superego, an inflamed conscience that blocks his instinctive drives:

> Because to be *bad*, Mother, that is the real struggle: to be bad – and to enjoy it! That is what makes men of us boys, Mother. But what my conscience, so-called, has done to my sexuality, my spontaneity, my courage! Never mind some of the things I try so hard to get away with – because the fact remains, *I don't*. I am marked like a road map from head to toe with my repressions. You can travel the length and breadth of my body over superhighways of shame and inhibition and fear. (p. 124)

There is something pathetic about Portnoy's hunger to be bad, as if only through being bad could he be truly potent.

Later on when he meets 'the old circle-jerker himself, Mr. Mandel', he wonders how such a bad boy, without the benefits of a good upbringing, could still be alive and flourishing. And his friend Smolka is apparently a professor at Princeton – Portnoy's gut reaction is one of shocked incredulity:

> But can't be! Without hot tomato soup for lunch on freezing afternoons? Who slept in those putrid pajamas? The owner of all those red rubber thimbles with the angry little spiky projections that he told us drove the girls up the walls of Paris? . . . I simply cannot believe in

the survival, let alone the middle-class success, of these two bad boys. (p. 176)

As an adult, Portnoy is still spontaneously reacting according to his mother's values, and that is why the life of sin is cloaked in such tremendously appealing terms. Alex is still a fearful adolescent who can never fully accommodate himself to guilty pleasures. In order for them to be pleasurable, they must be guilty, and sex must be dirty in order to be exciting. Alex needs to feel that he is actively degrading the world of his mother, but in actuality he can never degrade it enough to satisfy his prurient fantasies. Sexual reality always compares unfavorably with the sexual imagination, and Alex is doomed to a life of bitter disappointment.

His compulsive masturbation is deeply ambivalent. His pleasure is full of guilt and is intimately related to incestuous impulses toward his mother and sister. He whacks off and punishes himself at the same time. His penis is raw and swollen. By violating taboos, he is both rebelling and suffering for his rebellion. He masturbates in situations designed to produce a maximum of melodramatic effect; it is a kind of madness that comes over him to prove not only that he is a man, but also an entity separate from his mother's domination: 'My wang was all I really had that I could call my own' (p. 33). His greatest triumph and degradation occurs when he takes 'a big purplish piece of raw liver' from the refrigerator and masturbates with it:

> I believe that I have already confessed to the piece of liver that I bought in a butcher shop and banged behind a billboard on the way to a bar mitzvah lesson. Well, I wish to make a clean breast of it, Your Holiness. That – she – it wasn't my first piece. My first piece I had in the privacy of my own home, rolled round my cock in the bathroom at three-thirty – and then had again on the end of a fork, at five-thirty, along with the other members of that poor innocent family of mine. So. Now you know the worst thing I have ever done. I fucked my own family's dinner. (p. 134)

The desecration of food has deep anthropological roots, and Portnoy is trying hard to commit the Unpardonable Sin. His insane act of defiance has meaning only as a way of shaming himself before his ever-loving family. His secret guilt is both terrifying and exciting, because he has in some way outwitted his family, and especially his mother, who may exact a frightening penalty for his transgression. Remember her menacing, castrating presence, standing over him with a long breadknife when little Alex refuses to eat (p. 16).

Of course, Portnoy doesn't need Mrs Portnoy to punish him; he torments himself with the most horrible consequences brought on by his sexual excess. At one point he believes he has contracted cancer: 'All that pulling and tugging at my own flesh, all that friction, had given me an incurable disease' (p. 19). When he fantasizes about sex with Bubbles Girardi, he imagines that he gets syphilis and that his penis shrivels up and falls off. Portnoy stages a lurid confrontation with his family that is drenched in self-pitying thoughts of castration:

> 'What is that black plastic thing doing on the kitchen floor?' 'It's not a plastic one,' I say, and break into sobs. 'It's my own. I caught the syph from an eighteen-year-old Italian girl in Hillside, and now, now, I have no more p-p-p-penis!' 'His little thing,' screams my mother, 'that I used to tickle it to make him go wee-wee—' 'DON'T TOUCH IT NOBODY MOVE,' cries my father, for my mother seems about to leap forward onto the floor, like a woman into her husband's grave—'call—the Humane Society—' 'Like for a rabies *dog*?' she weeps . . . the scene fades quickly, for in a matter of seconds I am blind, and within the hour my brain is the consistency of hot Farina. (pp. 167–8)

Ironically, hot Farina is a nourishing cereal often fed to children when their stomachs can hold nothing else. It has a certain warm, sentimental resemblance to calf's liver, which is also extremely nutritious and which virtually all children loathe.

The most pathetic little Momma's boy in *Portnoy's Complaint* is Ronald Nimkin, 15 years old, a pianist with hands like José Iturbi, who hangs himself in the shower with a note pinned to his heavily starched sport shirt: '*Mrs. Blumenthal called. Please bring your mah-jongg rules for the game tonight*' (p. 120). To the ladies in the building the suicide is incomprehensible: 'You couldn't look for a boy more in love with his mother than Ronald!' (p. 97) but to Alex the death of Ronald Nimkin represents his own daily dying. He can only escape Ronald's fate by asserting his sexual independence:

> Stop already *hocking* us to be *good*! *hocking* us to be *nice*! Just leave us alone, God damn it, to pull our little dongs in peace and think our little selfish thoughts – stop already with the respectabilizing of our hands and our tushies and our mouths! Fuck the vitamins and the cod liver oil! Just give us each day our daily flesh! (p. 122)

This too is pathetic in its way, but it keeps Portnoy alive. His cousin Heshie, who knuckles under to his family about marrying a Christian drum majorette, Alice Dembosky, manages to get killed in the war and lose any chance of happiness, even with a dumb but sexy Polish girl. This is a sobering example to Alex. Death comes from respectability, doing the right thing, being dignified, sacrificing yourself, whereas life means following your instincts, enjoying yourself and, especially, indulging in frequent sex. In the narrow symbolic confines of *Portnoy's Complaint*, the chief metaphysical problems seem to be preserving your integrity and staying alive.

In *Fear of Flying*, Erica Jong makes a too easy dismissal of Philip Roth and his Jewish consciousness in *Portnoy's Complaint*:

> When I think of my mother I envy Alexander Portnoy. If only I had a *real* Jewish mother – easily pigeonholed and filed away – a real literary property. (I am always envying writers their relatives: Nabokov and Lowell and Tucci with their closets full of elegant aristocratic skeletons,

Roth and Bellow and Friedman with their pop parents, sticky as Passover wine, greasy as matzoh-ball soup.) (p. 147)

Is Mrs Portnoy 'a real literary property', with comic-strip Jewish traits? I think not, because we feel her tremendous and threatening lovableness throughout the novel. She is a complex character and not simply a collection of stereotyped Jewish characteristics. Despite the difference in social standing – Isadora's mother is upper middle class, while Alex's mother is lower, lower middle class – both Jewish mothers have a good deal in common. They both fill their children with an impossible sense of guilt that disables them from any easy enjoyment of life. Life is not made for pleasure but for accomplishments, and success is predicated on the sublimation of animal urges. Sex is for the mindless and untalented, a showy form of exhibitionism that has nothing to do with the real purpose of life.

Isadora is constantly struggling with her Jewish guilt, which she mistakenly tries to cure by a self-conscious and cultivated whorishness. Her chief sexual failures seem to lie in the domain of mock-nymphomania, especially with the psychiatrist Adrian Goodlove, whom she can never properly arouse. Like Portnoy, Isadora needs to feel guilty in order to survive, and both characters feel an additional pang because they never feel guilty enough. Ideally, Isadora sees herself as

a kind of Jewish Griselda [Patient Griselda of legend and Chaucer's 'Clerk's Tale']. She is Ruth and Esther and Jesus and Mary rolled into one. She always turns the other cheek. She is a vehicle, a vessel, with no needs or desires of her own. When her husband beats her, she understands him. When he is sick, she nurses him. When the children are sick, she nurses them. She cooks, keeps house, runs the store, keeps the books, listens to everyone's problems, visits the cemetery, weeds the graves, plants the garden, scrubs the floors, and sits quietly on the upper balcony of the synagogue while the men recite prayers about the inferiority of women. She is capable of absolutely everything except self-preservation. And secretly, I am always ashamed of myself for not being her. (p. 210)

This image, of course, has no relation to Mrs Portnoy either – it is only true of some highly idealized image of self-sacrificing woman as martyr. Neither Isadora nor Alex Portnoy ever forgets to pay lip service to guilt; they both wallow in it with a sticky self-pity. But we discover that these insistent, self-abasing declarations are a necessary form of self-inflation, without which both Alex and Isadora could never be permitted their full measure of self-indulgent irresponsibility.

It is important to recognize that Alex and Isadora play at guilt. They need to conceive themselves as children who have not lived up to parental ideals in order to have it both ways – that is, they are free to act out all the urgings of an infantile sexuality if only they feel guilty enough about it. In this bizarre equilibrium, guilt releases the participants from their hot and heavy repressions, so that pleasure (and especially sexual pleasure) can only be manufactured out of guilt. When, from conventional moral scruples about incest, Isadora refuses a much-desired bout of fellatio with her Arabic brother-in-law, she rationalizes her hesitations in terms of an irrational guilt:

> What a disproportionate sense of guilt *I* had over all my petty sexual transgressions! Yet there were people in the world, plenty of them, who did what they felt like and never had a moment's guilt over it – as long as they didn't get caught. Why had I been cursed with such a hypertrophied superego? Was it just being Jewish? What did Moses *do* for the Jews anyway by leading them out of Egypt and giving them the concept of one God, matzoh-ball soup, and everlasting guilt? (p. 245)

A guiltless, spontaneous sexuality becomes the ideal of the guilty, who seem to forget that it is their guilt that endows forbidden sexuality with such exciting resonance. It is only through guilt that sex can be felt so intensely, since guilt makes sex a cultural, ideational, cognitive artifact and not simply a physical transaction.

The longing Portnoy feels for *shikses* is obviously a cultural expression of guilt – remember that the state of Israel renders him totally impotent. The heart of Portnoy's Complaint is that he can only have sex with Christian girls, who represent the unkosher, ritually unclean and forbidden meats that he as a Jew has vowed never to touch – never to eat, we should say, because there is a basic pun throughout the novel on cunnilingus/fellatio and the violation of the dietary laws. It is because Mrs Portnoy's values are so overwhelmingly anchored in food and eating that Alex is so preoccupied with oral sex, which is his symbolic junk food (*chazerai*) by which he defies parental prohibitions. Orality is associated with generosity and giving and makes an important link with the instinctual life, of which sex, at least in this novel, is the chief expression.

Portnoy's frenzied whacking off on the 107 bus to Newark is directly attributable to his having eaten lobster, a crustacean also vividly involved in a traumatic, quasi-sexual episode of Mrs Portnoy earlier in the book. 'There are plenty of good things to eat in the world, Alex, without eating a thing like a lobster and running the risk of having paralyzed hands for the rest of your life' (p. 94). And 'Even in the Chinese restaurant, where the Lord has lifted the ban on pork dishes for the obedient children of Israel, the eating of lobster Cantonese is considered by God (Whose mouthpiece on earth, in matters pertaining to food, is my Mom) to be totally out of the question' (p. 90). Thus the eating of the unkosher lobster, even with his sister and her fiancé, Morty Feibish, in a restaurant at Sheepshead Bay (undoubtedly Lundy's) evokes strange, forbidden desires in Alex:

> Now, maybe the lobster is what did it. That taboo so easily and simply broken, confidence may have been given to the whole slimy, suicidal Dionysian side of my nature; the

lesson may have been learned that to break the law, all you have to do is – just go ahead and break it! All you have to do is stop trembling and quaking and finding it unimaginable and beyond you: all you have to do, *is do it*! What else, I ask you, were all those prohibitive dietary rules and regulations all about to begin with, what else but to give us little Jewish children practice in being repressed? . . . Why else the kosher soap and salt? Why else, I ask you, but to remind us three times a day that life is boundaries and restrictions if it's anything, hundreds of thousands of little rules laid down by none other than None Other. (pp. 79–80)

So Portnoy interprets his precarious masturbation on the 107 bus, next to a *shikse* in 'tartan skirt folds', as an act of daring defiance of the dietary laws and all they represent.

Food is moralized and allegorized in this book, making eating and sex parallel activities:

Renunciation is all, cries the koshered and bloodless piece of steak my family and I sit down to eat at dinner time. Self-control, sobriety, sanctions – this is the key to a human life, saith all those endless dietary laws. Let the *goyim* sink *their* teeth into whatever lowly creature crawls and grunts across the face of the dirty earth, we will not contaminate our humanity thus. (pp. 80–1)

Portnoy's life is steeped in a Manichean dualism: to be a Jew is to be moral, civilized and tame; to be a Christan (*goy*) is to be sexual, unthinking and powerfully instinctive. For little Alex, the Christian world is stuffed full of alluring, heroic images that he wants to seize by cunning and force. In food terms, these large symbolic domains are defined naively; simply by eating unkosher food one introverts the values of the Christian world:

For look at Alex himself, the subject of *our* every syllable – age fifteen, he sucks one night on a lobster's claw and within the hour his cock is out and aimed at a *shikse* on a

Public Service bus. And his superior Jewish brain might
as well be *made* of *matzoh brei*! (p. 82)

The intellect destroying effect of eating lobster is almost
chemical; within the hour the poison is already working.
The unkosher, Christianized lobster becomes a heroic
image of male sexuality, and Portnoy, like Prufrock, might
wish to be 'a pair of rugged claws/Scuttling across the floors
of silent seas' (T.S. Eliot, 'The Love Song of J. Alfred Prufrock').

Portnoy's longing to be part of the Christian world also
expresses a desire to be part of that larger America that is
outside the Jewish ghetto of Newark. E. M. Forster's phrase,
'only connect', applies with some vividness and wordplay to
Alex, who is seeking connection with a reality outside the
narrow sphere of his home. Late in the novel, after a series
of sexual triumphs over notable *shikses*, Portnoy understands that his social and sexual impulses have become
strangely merged: 'What I'm saying, Doctor, is that I don't
seem to stick my dick up these girls, as much as I stick it up
their backgrounds – as though through fucking I will discover America. *Conquer* America – maybe that's more like it'
(p. 235). 'As though through fucking I will discover
America' sounds like the theme of Nabokov's *Lolita*, as
Humbert Humbert and his child prodigy/whore wander
through an eroticized America drenched in kitsch. It is only
through sex that Portnoy can connect with the country of his
birth from which he has been alienated. This fantasy
America is pre-eminently a WASP rather than an ethnic
country, where the Jew is the archetypal outsider who forces
his way in by sexual attraction alone. For Portnoy, his prestigious, blond-haired and blue-eyed girl friends represent
his conquest of forbidden territory. He plays the bad-ass
Jewish stud who forces his women to indulge his sexual
whims, and especially his craving for oral sex. Portnoy is like
the Woody Allen stereotype of the timid macho, as in the
Humphrey Bogart pastiche of *Play It Again Sam*. He is con-
queror and conquered at the same time. He is the grotesque

patriot who wants what's coming to him: '*My* G.I. bill – real American ass! The cunt in country – 'tis of thee!' (p. 236). The hysterical Portnoy is determined to claim his sexual birthright.

Isadora is less alienated from her America, yet she is acutely aware of her need to declare her sexual independence from the marketplace definition of what it means to be a woman. Some of the best writing in *Fear of Flying* is a parody of mediaspeak and psychobabble:

> What all the ads and all the whoreoscopes seemed to imply was that if only you were narcissistic *enough*, if only you took proper care of your smells, your hair, your boobs, your eyelashes, your armpits, your crotch, your stars, your scars, and your choice of Scotch in bars – you would meet a beautiful, powerful, potent, and rich man who would satisfy every longing, fill every hole, make your heart skip a beat (or stand still), make you misty, and fly you to the moon (preferably on gossamer wings), where you would live totally satisfied forever. . . . Underneath it all, you longed to be annihilated by love, to be swept off your feet, to be filled up by a giant prick spouting sperm, soapsuds, silks and satins, and of course, money. (pp. 9–10)

Isadora is sensitive to the emotional clichés of the ladies' magazines, and she feels herself in rebellion against that same American way of life that Alex Portnoy finds romantically closed to him:

> I knew my itches were un-American – and that made things *still* worse. It is heresy in America to embrace any way of life except as half of a couple. Solitude is un-American. It may be condoned in a man – especially if he is a 'glamorous bachelor' who 'dates starlets' during a brief interval between marriages. But a woman is always presumed to be alone as a result of abandonment, not choice. And she is treated that way: as a pariah. . . . Her friends, her family, her fellow workers never let her

forget that her husbandlessness, her childlessness – her *selfishness*, in short – is a reproach to the American way of life. (pp. 10–11)

'Selfishness' is, in fact, Sophie Portnoy's word for her son's failure to settle down and produce offspring. As a writer, Isadora is already defying the American stereotypes for a creative woman – a dress designer or fashion photographer would suit the stereotype better than a writer – and it becomes clear from *How to Save Your Own Life* (1977), an overlapping sequel to *Fear of Flying*, that Bennett takes a mistress at the very moment that Isadora is most deeply immersed in her writing career. For her husband, to be a writer is somehow to deny being a woman, and he acts to console himself for the loss of his wife to literature.

Isadora is, of course, a hopeless romantic. In Vienna she deserts her husband for his vague and rootless antitype, Adrian Goodlove, also a psychiatrist, but hedonistic, permissive and overwhelmingly narcissistic: 'When I threw in my lot with Adrian Goodlove, I entered a world in which the rules we lived by were his rules – although, of course, he pretended there *were* no rules' (p. 177). She pursues his 'eternal limp prick' (p. 89) with a vain fervor, since 'the very intensity of my need canceled out his. The more I showed my passion, the cooler he became' (p. 274).

Isadora's sexual scenario is played out against American values, and especially the glossy, media values of a consumerist culture:

I suddenly had a passion to *be* that ordinary girl. To be that good little housewife, that glorified American mother, that mascot from *Mademoiselle*, that matron from *McCall's*, that cutie from *Cosmo*, that girl with the Good Housekeeping Seal tattooed on her ass and advertising jingles programmed in her brain. *That* was the solution! To be ordinary! To be unexotic! To be content with compromise and TV dinners and 'Can This Marriage Be Saved?' I had a fantasy then of myself as a happy housewife. A fantasy straight out of an adman's little brain. Me

in apron and gingham shirtwaist waiting on my husband
and kiddies while the omnipresent TV set sings out the
virtues of the American home and the American slave-
wife with her tiny befuddled brain. (p. 253)

There is a touch of envy and longing in all of this, as Isadora
sees the advantages of being a befuddled little slave-wife like
her sister Randy. Isadora feels intensely guilty and bitchy
that her Great Sexual Adventure has turned out so tawdry.
She flirts with being ordinary because she is so firmly convinced that she is as extraordinary as her mother could wish
her. She has been chosen for a destiny, creative and sexual,
that is grandly set apart from the American way of life. What
could be more romantically American than to imagine oneself as the Great Gatsby of fucking?

Portnoy imagines grandly, too, and in his mind's eye he
does doughty deeds with *shikses* too numerous to mention.
For all his masochistic self-pity, Portnoy's sexual fantasies are
full of derring-do and a hard, aggressive degradation of the
world he sets out to conquer. Devaluation and defloration
go together. The Yiddish in the novel is a vehicle for these
ambivalent longings, a secret, ironic language as in Peter
Brook's work and in Ted Hughes' *Orghast*, a synthetic word
system expressing the emotions of phonetic association. In
Brook's *Ik*, the made-up language also has a perfect conso-
nance with the meanings it expresses – it *is* those meanings.

For Portnoy, the Yiddish word *shikse* means a non-Jewish
girl, but it is not a neutral term. It identifies the non-Jewish
woman in relation to a Jewish man, and it carries strong
connotations of a sexually attractive but mindless woman.
Shikse is much more specific than the generalized word *goy*
for gentile, because a *shikse* is the wonderfully exciting
woman you are forbidden to marry. Alice Dembosky, 'in her
tiny white skirt with the white satin bloomers, and the white
boots that come midway up the muscle of her lean, strong
calves', is described as 'blatantly a shikse' (p. 54), which
seems to mean that only a *shikse* would aspire to be head
drum majorette of the high school band. This is pure

goyische naches (p. 55), or the kind of pleasure only a Christian desires out of life, like waiting to see the Kaiser in the rain. Yiddish is a splendid language of veiled contempt. *Ven der putz shteht, ligt der sechel in drerd* is a much-quoted apothegm in *Portnoy's Complaint*, translated by Alex as: 'When the prick stands up, the brains get buried in the ground!' (p. 128) – *in dred* is part of the mild curse, *geh in dred*, meaning 'go to hell'. It is a typically Yiddish dualism to contrast the workings of the *putz* (prick) with those of the *sechel* (brains, wisdom, good sense). In this unbridgeable dichotomy, the *putz* easily obliterates any trace of *sechel* that may remain. The proud self-contempt of the proverb is almost reassuring.

Sexual invective endows *Portnoy's Complaint* with comic vitality. It is a Rabelaisian book because it is so copious and uninhibited in its expression of vital energies. There is no holding back in Alex Portnoy's torrential confessions to his psychoanalyst, who listens patiently from the beginning of the book to the end and has only one line himself, the *punch line*: 'So [said the doctor]. Now vee may perhaps to begin. Yes?' (p. 274). The whole book is only the worthless ravings of a neurotic patient, who must dispose of all his garbage before the serious business of psychotherapy can begin. It is the wildness of *Portnoy's Complaint* that has endeared this book to so many readers, who participate in the frenzied and compulsive barrage of sex and aggression. The book offers release for our own bottled guilts about dirty words, masturbation, racial prejudices and other censored materials of the fantasy life.

It is a gust of fresh air, for example, to hear all the most dreaded street-words of mindless anti-Semitism from the soiled lips of Bubbles Girardi, who is infuriated that Portnoy has just ejaculated all over the living-room furniture:

> 'Son of a bitch kike!' Bubbles screams. 'You got gissum all over the couch! And the walls! And the lamp!'
> 'I got it in my eye! And don't you say kike to me, you!'
> 'You *are* a kike, Kike! You got it all over everything, you mocky son of a bitch! Look at the doilies!' (p. 180)

We are jolted by Bubbles' concern for the doilies, which is the least of Alex's worries at this moment – he is sure that he is going blind from sperm in the eye. But Bubbles has been infuriated beyond all measure, and the hot lava of anti-Semitism keeps pouring out:

> 'Sheeny!' she is screaming. 'Hebe! You can't even come off unless you pull your own pudding, cheap bastard fairy Jew!' (p. 181)

Portnoy's less sensitive friend, Mandel, is unmoved by the revelation that Bubbles is anti-Semitic: 'Mandel, the next day tells me that within half an hour after my frenetic departure, Bubbles was down on her fucking dago knees sucking his cock' (p. 182). Mandel is indifferent to abstractions like anti-Semitism:

> 'She called me a kike!' I answer self-righteously. 'I thought I was blind. Look, she's anti-Semitic, Ba-ba-lu.'
> 'Yeah, what do I give a shit?' says Mandel. Actually I don't think he knows what anti-Semitic means. 'All I know is I got laid, *twice*.' (p. 182)

Portnoy is doomed to be continuously tantalized and frustrated, because he can never shake off the values of his mother, his father and his forefathers. He can never enjoy sex for its own sake, juicy and non-meaningful. His elaborate and tormented language is a way of coping with the physical pleasure that slips out of his grasp. Like Isadora in *Fear of Flying*, Alex Portnoy is a magnificent talker, and exhorter, and Dionysiac artist with words because the more direct reality eludes him.

7 PERFORMATIVE SEX AND THE VALUES OF A CONSUMERIST CULTURE: *Blue Skies, No Candy; Candy* and *Lolita*

S EXUAL literature is a vehicle for cultural mythology. Sex can mean whatever any particular society at any given moment in history wants it to mean. Physiology only establishes the parameters, and even sexual physiology has its fashionable concerns – witness the tremendous contemporary interest in female orgasm, specifically clitoral orgasm. There is a sociology of sexual mores and sexual tastes that can be studied historically in its evolving patterns. The great sexual revolution of the 1960s has more or less run its course, and it is now difficult to find most of that great avalanche of erotic books that were popularly reprinted for the first time – and never reprinted again. Whether or not the number of X-rated movies in circulation has declined (a statistic disputed by Women Against Pornography), obligatory scenes of sex and nudity are no longer so fashionably obligatory in movies of general distribution. Bra-less women and see-through blouses and micro-mini skirts seem to have receded from public display. Flamboyant nudity (or near nudity) has declared its right to be and quietly disappeared without ever establishing its claim to First Amendment guarantees. Apparently the Constitution does not recognize nudity as a form of protected self-expression.

Sexuality is one among many products of a consumerist society. *Playboy, Penthouse, Hustler* and their imitators use sex to sell advertising. The pleasant fantasies evoked by naked men and women put the reader in the right mood to buy the luxury products of an affluent society: expensive shoes, vacations, resort wear, perfumes and deodorants, sporting goods, health club memberships and all the paraphernalia of conspicuous consumption and upward mobility. A frank interest in sex is equated with boldness of imagination, originality of lifestyle, effervescent hedonism and a general commitment to extroverted, healthy values. It is very American to be concerned with high-quality performance, whether in stereo equipment, scuba diving gear, sports cars or sex. Suddenly, everything is officially permitted and encouraged, there is no guilt, and men and women can enjoy each other's bodies as well as each other's high-polish omelet pans, Yucatan hammocks and vintage California wines. No sweat. There is suddenly a blizzard of sexual self-help books designed to improve the quality and frequency of your orgasm, introduce you to copulatory postures known only in the brothels of Hong Kong, and answer everything you always wanted to know about sex but were afraid to ask. One can become a connoisseur in sex just as one can become a gourmet, an oenophile and almost a tennis pro. All that is required is application, study, practice and ample resources to pursue one's leisure-time interests.

We have been sketching a popular sexual mythology that has little or nothing to do with real sex with live human partners. This is fantasy, wish-fulfillment sex by which you not only satisfy all of your physical cravings, but also your overpowering impulse to get ahead in life, be one of the boys or girls and make a name for yourself. Gael Greene's recent novel, *Blue Skies, No Candy* (1976), is a delightful expression of these performative, consumerist values, and a spoof of that chic, moneyed, slick and sleek society it represents. Sex is the lingua franca that draws the beautiful people together. It is the one motive that can be counted on in a society insanely devoted to self-expression and pleasure. Gael Greene's heroine, Kate Alexander, the fabulous screenwriter, is aging – she is 40 – but still extraordinarily pneumatic (to use Aldous Huxley's term for sex appeal in *Brave New World*). She is always expensively dressed, perfectly made up, never at a loss for words (especially words that will sell her product) and always ready for erotic dalliance accompanied by gourmet food and vintage wines.

At the end of the novel, when Kate has been abandoned by both her adorable husband Jamie and her masterful lover Jason, the Cowboy, Kate suddenly imagines the end of the world and the strenuous preparations she will have to make for that event:

> I suppose this is how I will function if they ever announce the world is about to end. A quick trip to M. Marc for a comb-out. A few minutes of indecision at the closet. Shall I be tailored and elegant or soft, monochromatic or subtly sexy, irrepressibly earthy? How will we meet Armageddon, barefoot with toes painted Teddy Bear rose or in our Chelsea Cobbler boots, kicking to the end? (pp. 343–4)

Kate is disarmingly theatrical at all times; it is her only form of spontaneity.

Gael Greene's heroine is almost entirely a sensual creature, and she is always a public person. She is conscious of playing to an audience, especially a movie audience, and her medium is the media. She is always aware of publicity, public relations, image, as defined and marketable commodities. Her own personal catastrophe at the end of the novel is hardly personal at all. Her secretary is weeping, but the heroic Kate will see it through:

> Jesus Christ, what is this? A goddam fucking soap opera? I've just got to get through today and tomorrow. Jamie loves me. He'll come back. He came back that other time. Holly, be cool and cheerful. Be Anne Baxter in *All About Eve*, if you like. (pp. 344–5)

There is a thin line separating television and the movies and real life, and it is difficult to discern which is more authentic.

Kate is thoroughly histrionic in her sincerity. In her crisis, she wants to come to grips with things as they actually are: 'And I have crawled into my bed-nest with a notebook to make a list of deeply perceptive, humble, witty, irreverent things I want to say to *Time*' (p. 345). Only acknowledged celebrities speak directly to *Time* magazine; their private disasters are matters of public interest. Kate does not wallow for long in personal grief. She is soon preparing to meet Michael at the Algonquin for a vigorous afternoon of sadomasochistic games: 'a good fuck always agrees with me. Great fucking is a better beauty pickup than silicone or estrogen or sleep. Too bad Estée Lauder can't put it in a bottle' (p. 345).

So ends the novel and Kate's denouement, with sexual/moral advice and specific brand names of fashionable products. *Blue Skies, No Candy* levitates its readers with a panoply of 'in' allusions: 'Gucci shoulder bag. Hermes attaché case' (p. 17); 'The room is heavy with Brut' (p. 18); the George V hotel in Paris (p. 207); Maxwell's Plum (p. 211); 'It's all wonderfully Henri Bendel' (p. 225); 'He loves our rented Mercedes' (p. 238); 'He has his hands between my legs in the garden of the Restaurant de la Pyramide in Vienne' (p. 251); 'This morning I couldn't button the waistband on my St Laurent pants' (p. 252); 'Diane drives an orchid Camaro, custom paint job' (p. 263); 'Jason is angry with me because I didn't call ahead from Paris to reserve a room at Baumanière' (p. 267). Our heroine proves to be an extraordinary name-dropper.

Kate invests a small fortune on clothes that will be appropriate for her sexual escapade with the Cowboy in France. Everything is specified with the full verisimilitude of ladies' homemaker magazines such as *Cosmopolitan* and *Redbook* (which are craftily disguised repositories of domestic erotica):

Shopping for France and adventure. A rampage through Altman's lingerie department, rejecting lacy black nighties. No, it must be sheer, simple and see-through. Spending an absolutely unprecedented seventy-five dollars for a pale blue nightgown by Dior, cut square and low. Buying a dozen pairs of bikini panties and all-lace bras, and rosy satin deshabille slit right up to here, fantasizing rose satin lifting, lace-wrapped breasts being bared, Frederick's of Hollywood bikinis being ripped away. Turned on hot and creaming in a spartan Altman's fitting room, behind the green door. (pp. 201–2)

Behind the Green Door is, of course, the X-rated movie with Marilyn Chambers, the Ivory Snow girl, 99.44 per cent pure.

The pale blue Dior nightgown reappears in a sexy scene in the stone annex at Beaumanière in France: 'The blue Dior nightgown is different from anything I've worn. Rather serious, with an edge of lace barely covering the aureole of my breasts. He watches' (pp. 273–4). This is clearly a costume novel, in which clothes, perfumes, accessories and furnishings figure as importantly as in *Story of O*. The Dior nightgown is a great success and well worth the 'absolutely unprecedented' sum Kate pays for it: 'He drops the straps of my gown, kisses both breasts, drops Dior's best intentions into a tangle of blue nylon on the floor' (p. 274). The sexual props are perfect, and Kate has prepared for her big scene with consummate artistry. Her consumerist instinct not to compromise with quality – it cost a lot but it's worth it – has once more been vindicated.

Kate's sexual fantasies are like the scenarios of dirty movies, with all the details vividly specified. The abundance of detail makes *Blue Skies, No Candy* teeter on the edge of parody, like Terry Southern's aimlessly uninhibited romp, *Blue Movie* (1971). Gael Greene manages to leave nothing out, so that her super-sexual novel is also a peep into the cornucopia of life as it is lived on Central Park West and the Upper West Side of New York – the aerodrome itself of Isadora Wing's *Fear of Flying*. Gael Greene even manages a plug for Zabar's, the fabulous delicatessen on Broadway between 80th and 81st Streets:

I can't quite believe it. Kate Alexander of Central Park West on a ranch somewhere outside of Houston [where the Cowboy wants to take her]. How do people find the bare minimal comforts of life west of the Hudson? What do they do for Scotch salmon and Moishe's black pumpernickel without Zabar's? (p. 295)

What gives *Blue Skies, No Candy* its charm is not so much the sex itself, which is often tedious, but the aura of consumerist chic in which the sex is wrapped. It is not surprising that Gael Greene, a trenchant restaurant critic for *New York* magazine, should put such strong emphasis on food. Her characters seem to divide their time between copulating and eating. The food references are wonderfully knowledgeable. Thus when Jamie walks out on her, Kate introduces a 'macabre gastronomic touch': 'Jamie's prized Rudolph Stanish omelet pan. I hid it when he packed. I won't let him make perfect omelets for some twenty-three-old morally superior home-destroyer who wouldn't know a perfect omelet anyway' (p. 306). Gastronomic and sexual values are amusingly equated, and Kate asserts her assured superiority in terms of perfect omelets.

In a cozy sexual scene with Jamie early in the novel, they send out for pizza to the fashionable Goldberg's Pizzeria on the East Side, which doesn't ordinarily deliver to the West Side. The husband–wife dialogue that follows is richly camp and intimate:

> 'Let's have a special wine, Jamie. Something really stirring. Something too grand for pizza. Something that will move me to tears. After all, this is a landmark pizza.'
> Jamie comes back in a paint-stained sweatshirt with a bottle from the wine closet. ' '62 La Gaffelière Naudes,' he says. 'An insouciant Saint-Émilion to complement Madame's mozzarella.'
> 'Can a Saint-Émilion be insouciant, Jamie?'
> 'I don't know, Rabbit. I'm just faking it like everyone else.' (pp. 46–7)

The parody of wine snobbery cuts both ways, since Jamie

and Kate are opening a fine, vintage Bordeaux to drink with pizza and also making fun of their self-indulgence.

Food delineates a special erotic bond between Kate and Jamie; Jamie's attraction is strongly indicated in his cooking:

> Jamie's French toast is always perfect, sodden with egg and golden brown, sometimes dusted with sugar, sometimes pressed together with nutty yellow fontina or even brie. Once he made French toast of a tunafish sandwich. That is his bizarre bent. Apricots in shrimp curry. Foie gras tucked inside chicken Kiev. Sometimes his madness is brilliant. Green crêpes filled with sour cream and a puree of avocado. And his chocolate rum milk shakes are demonic. (pp. 70–1)

On food criteria, however, the Cowboy doesn't qualify:

> He prefers white wine, very cold, not too dry. And sweet innocent white cheese. Or gruyère. The familiar. He wants to eat his sausage with a fork. He watches me tear off a hunk of the bread. He asks for a bread knife. He has so much to learn. Kate smiles. (p. 222)

Why does Kate smile? Is it because she knows secretly that a man who doesn't understand and savor food cannot ultimately be a good lover? As devotees of the 'soaps', we know from the Cowboy's gaucherie with food that Kate cannot find true happiness with Jason and that she will eventually get back with Jamie.

Kate understands her own sexuality in food terms, as in the following passage, where the bread simile is revealing:

> Should I lie on my back with my legs spread prettily, showing the pink, rubbing my clitoris and playing with my nipples? Acting out fantasies is basically improvisational. It's like making bread the first time. You read all the instructions and you know the dough is going to double in bulk but till you get in there and punch it back into shape, you can't even guess. (pp. 142–3)

Does this image turn on the yeasty, erectile power of bread?

It is a wonderfully earthy image for masturbation – domestic and close to home.

It takes a certain boldness for Gael Greene to be so old-fashioned in her representation of female sexuality. She is distinctly hostile to women's liberation views. In her tax-deductible lunch with Noni Gelfan at Maxwell's Plum, Kate objects to ideas attributed to Gloria Steinem about body hair and men. Noni accuses Kate of having the reputation of being an 'Aunt Tom':

> 'Maybe in some nutty way, sex is to woman what alcohol is to the alcoholic. In order to be free, perhaps you've got to eliminate sex from your life entirely.'
>
> 'Sex is the last thing I'm eliminating. The only thing I'm eliminating is body hair. What is existence without sex, Noni? What is life without men?' (p. 119)

One can understand why, just before this, Kate thinks that she must renew her subscription to *Vogue*. She is not afraid of men, and she asserts views that are anathema to the Women's Movement. She lives in a distinctly material world, in which the erotic is only an extension of other pleasures of the senses. In this respect Kate comes right out of the pages of Henry Miller, although her snobbery and fashionableness are very different from Miller's indiscriminate all-inclusiveness.

In a scene with her feminist friends, Kate shocks them all by insisting on her need to be a sex object:

> 'But I want to be possessed,' says Kate. 'I like being a sex object. I get nervous when I'm with a man who doesn't see me as a sex object. In the movie world, in the business world, a successful woman sometimes stops being seen as a woman. Or else she's seen as a mutant creature, a woman with balls.' (p. 157)

Kate goes further by justifying her rape fantasy, which is not even a fantasy:

> Once I needed to be raped . . . when I lost my virginity on the floor of a darkroom, that was rape. I didn't want to.

He forced me. I was grateful that he did. I was furious, thought I was furious at the moment, but I was free to be myself. Rape, a kind of a rape, was the only way it was going to happen. I was a senior in high school, ravenous for sex, still, determined to be a virgin on my wedding night. All the forces of evil were after me, bulging trousers, my own heat, D. H. Lawrence. (p. 158)

It is amusing to see D. H. Lawrence – presumably the Lawrence of *Lady Chatterley's Lover* – among the forces of evil conspiring Kate's defloration. This passage is aggressively opposed to feminist values, and it looks as if Gael Greene enjoys taking on the whole Women's Movement.

There is a great deal of sadomasochistic sex in *Blue Skies, No Candy*. It is part of erotic games, including bondage and discipline, with Michael, Jamie and Jason. This aspect of the novel deepens our understanding of Kate's ideas about rape. She admits to having a copy of *Story of O* 'tucked between my nightgowns', and she explains to an uncomprehending Cowboy how the woman's submission is a paradox:

To be penetrated, controlled, to be possessed. And yet always to emerge, still there, still me. . . . Penetration isn't only passive. . . . It can be aggressive. I take you into me, I ride you, devour you. . . . I'm in control. . . . Does he feel the power I have encircling his cock – the teeth little boys imagine we hide inside down there? Will I give it back? Will it be there when I let it go and he returns from his *petite mort* – as the French call orgasm, the little death? (pp. 257–8)

These passages are close in spirit to Pauline Réage and Jean de Berg, and throughout the novel Kate toys with Gothic fantasies: 'It's a game and it's real. The stranger is biting my neck, shaking me, entering me with nasty fingers, a rough dream demon, pulling my hair, shoving his cock into my mouth, holding wrists to the bed, making me a prisoner' (p. 314).

Kate is a fantasizer, a fictionalizer, a screenwriter by profession. She invents sex to entertain herself. She writes parts for herself in her own erotic movies, so that the line between fiction and real life is blurred. In *Blue Skies, No Candy* the extended, straight and unimaginative sex with the Cowboy is the weakest part of the book, whereas the earlier scenes with a variety of improbable lovers have the wit and spice of good scripts that will make even better movies. There is always a doubleness of perspective about Kate – she is both avid participant in and satirical observer of her own sexual capers, in which she is heaving with passion and laughing at herself at the same time.

The sadomasochistic games can force fantasy and reality into an unstable, colloidal mixture, as in Kate's description of her lover Michael:

> Well, now Michael puts on his skin-grazing black leather jeans with the grin of zippers up the calves. He couldn't get into them otherwise. And the shiny black tunic with the hardware that makes me think of whips and chains. He tilts a shiny lizard-skin cap at a menacing angle on his straw-blond hair. His goggles are mirror so you can't peer in to see if maybe, please, Michael's just kidding. I'm too numb to laugh. Then he's gone. Michael is my Hell's Angel gangbang. (p. 15)

Thus Michael equilibrates between the worlds of a lush copywriter making scads of money and of a tough stud in leather who enslaves his women. Which scene is more theatrical? When Kate thinks of the hard-core skin flick she is in, her only reaction is humor: 'I am just your everyday late-blooming adulteress and when this scene gets really kinky, I have to grit my teeth to keep from laughing' (p. 11). It is kinky and it is funny. The two categories do not exclude each other as they do in hard-core, drugstore pornography, which caters solely to fantasy.

In lush, Technicolor italics, Kate re-runs old movies in her head in which she casts herself as the leading lady. This is straight parody that develops the double perspective of

Kate as observer and observed. At the end of the novel she is Scarlett O'Hara in *Gone with the Wind*:

> *I am standing here in the burned-out hulk of Tara with all my faithful darkies gathered about me. Minnie, Malcolm X, Martin Luther King, and Sidney Poitier. Sidney is slicing a watermelon. Everyone hums a mournful hymn. Holly is trying to lace me into my girdle.*
>
> *'You gwine have to lay off them chocolate mousses, Miz Scarlett.'*
>
> *'I'm leaving, Scarlett,' says Jamie* [as Rhett Butler].
>
> *'No. Oh my darling, if you go, what shall I do?'*
>
> *'My dear, I don't give a damn.'*
>
> *Holly jerks the strings tight.* (p. 346)

The melodramatic projection dissipates the pain of Jamie's departure. An earlier rape fantasy is a take-off on *Lawrence of Arabia*:

> *I stoop to pick up a piece of bright blue sea-glass, feeling as if I have been sloughing through the sands for days. My hood fallen low over my face. Katherine of Arabia.*
>
> *Suddenly Kate is surrounded by white-robed Arabs on horseback. She recognizes their faces. Joe Namath. Burt Reynolds. Hugh Hefner. Warren Beatty. Mick Jagger. They are going to rape her. Hefner rips open her burnoose. 'Not exactly your typical girl-next-door,' he says.* (p. 168)

In this super-macho assemblage, the threat is removed by the snappy dialogue, ending with Kate's climactic one-liner: *'I thought Rin Tin Tin was dead.'*

Kate sees her life unfolding as a movie. 'I am Catherine Deneuve in *Belle de Jour*. Can't stop. Can't get enough. I love it' (p. 51). Jason 'cuddles me with a look that makes me wonder if he isn't seeing Carroll Baker curled up in a baby crib' (p. 304) in *Baby Doll*. 'The three faces of Kate' after *The Three Faces of Eve*: 'Cunt, Baby Snooks and pussypie' (p. 304). Reality is essentially cinematic; at Fire Island the

> community has converged at the ferry like dozens of extras thronging to market in a De Mille epic, lovers

linked in the same consciously choreographed embrace, Romans, Christians, slaves and a sprinkling of concubines and offspring costumed by Edith Head, Levi and Giorgio de Sant'Angelo. (p. 125)

Kate sees herself and Jason in bed 'through the camera eye', and Kate's brain is busy manufacturing 'boffo one-liners' (p. 216) for the scene. There is no reality, even the most physical sexual reality, without fiction-making and artifice.

When Kate sees Jamie again after returning from France (and Jason), their meeting is overlaid by movie techniques and sample dialogue:

Oh, Jamie. Here we are hugging and sobbing and touching, the kind of leaky fumblings grown people do in real life. It would all be too slow, too boring for the screen. That's why we have the fades and dissolves and Godard leaps. To spare you. Let's get to the dialogue. He loves me. He'll never love anyone the way he loves me. No one will ever love him the way I love him. What we had was so special. There must be a way to save it. This is not crisp snappy dialogue. But it's us. I believe him. (pp. 330–1)

But the scene is falsified by the intrusive presence of other lovers. It is, literally, a sexual soap opera, rehearsing conventional postures and attitudes. It has no emotional depth.

The satirical brittleness and smartness of *Blue Skies, No Candy* owe an obvious debt to Terry Southern and Mason Hoffenberg's *Candy*, first published by the Olympia Press in Paris in 1958. Between *Candy* and *No Candy* there is a generation gap. *Candy* is a parody of Voltaire's *Candide* (1759) through the medium of the Eisenhower 1950s and the Cold War. Candy's bubbling optimism and sincerity – she too sees 'Blue skies . . . nothing but blue skies', as in the song – her heartfelt response to the needs of others (especially the underprivileged), make her a folk heroine like the comic-strip character, Little Orphan Annie. In fact, she tends to speak in perfect middle-American, homespun phrases:

'golly', 'gosh', 'darn' and 'N–O spells *no*'. Her 'Good grief, it's Daddy' at climactic moments echoes Little Orphan Annie's own exaggerated awe for her Daddy Warbucks, who is an Eisenhower surrogate and who would have been capable of saying, when he discovers his daughter in bed with the semi-literate Mexican gardener, '*You . . . You . . . You . . .* COMMUNIST!' (p. 43). Like Sade's Justine, who is also modeled on Voltaire's Candide, Candy goes through life doing good, but always finds her benevolence rewarded by strenuous intercourse and exploitation. Nothing that happens to her, however, can shake Candy's faith in virtue and the beatific vision.

Candy wants to be needed or needs to be wanted – it hardly matters, because the polite, moralistic formulas of middle-America are hollow abstractions. Candy disguises her own aching needs as a response to the needs of others. She becomes a sexual Florence Nightingale, who not only gives of herself, but herself too. Candy's thesis for Professor Mephesto, on which she receives an A-plus for obvious reasons, states her credo: 'To give of oneself – fully – is not merely a duty prescribed by an outmoded superstition, it is a beautiful and thrilling privilege' (p. 20). How splendidly ambiguous! Like everything in *Candy*, the passage is bathed in delicious *double entendre*. Candy Christian is the super-innocent whore, who, unlike Bunyan's Christian in *Pilgrim's Progress* (1678), sets out on her pilgrimage with naive faith in the goodness of man and a cunning and lubricious determination to take all experience at its face value. She is a non-psychological heroine, who willfully misunderstands everything that is happening to her. In the blizzard of Larger Significances and Spiritual Resonances, Candy can blissfully ignore the insanely erotic activities in which she is so vigorously engaged.

Candy is a quixotic and sexually picaresque novel which projects the heroine's incestuous attraction to a series of fatherly gurus: Professor Mephesto, her charismatic teacher; Uncle Jack, her father's adorable twin brother; Dr Irving Krankeit (*né* Semite), author of the anti-Lawrence

treatise, *Masturbation Now!*; Dr Howard Johns, your neigh-
borhood gynecologist; Pete Uspy, the Russian philanthrop-
ist of the Cracker Foundation; Grindle, his priapic associate,
and finally the dung- and ash-covered holy man whom
Candy meets in Calcutta and in Lhasa and who miraculously
proves to be her Daddy. For Candy spiritual communion
always turns up accompanied by sexual union.

In the first episode of the novel, Candy feels guilty that
she has not lived up to the literal meaning of her thesis with
Professor Mephesto: 'Selfish! Selfish! she was thinking of
herself. To be needed by this great man! And to be only
concerned with my material self! She was horribly ashamed.
How he needs me! And I deny him! *I deny him!* Oh, how did I
dare?' (pp. 25–6) A mean egotism is the ultimate negative in
Candy's world, since she has devoted her life to the good of
others. We seem to hear a distant parody of the hard self-
sacrifice in *Story of O*.

With Emmanuel the Mexican gardener, Candy decides to
give herself to compensate him for his life of ethnic depriva-
tion and to prove that not all Anglos are prejudiced like her
father. In the seduction scene Candy speaks with the absurd
flippancy of a sorority girl, mimicking Professor Mephesto's
own overheated, baroque clichés. She offers Emmanuel 'a
drop of sherry': 'I find it has body *and* edge. Not like tea, a
messy affair at best. Don't you agree?' (p. 34) To which the
astounded Mexican can only answer here (and elsewhere):
'Whot?' Candy wants to sacrifice herself, so she is genuinely
puzzled when she begins to feel sexual pleasure:

> 'Oh, you do need me so!' the closed-eyed girl murmured,
> as yet not feeling much of anything except the certainty
> of having to fit this abstraction to the case. But when the
> gardener's hand closed on her pelvis and into the damp,
> she stiffened slightly: she was quite prepared to undergo
> *pain* for him . . . but *pleasure* – she was not sure how that
> could be a part of the general picture. So she seized his
> hand and contented herself for the moment with the
> giving of her left breast, to which his mouth was fastened

in desperate sucking.

'Oh my baby, my baby,' she whispered, stroking his head; but the hot insulting hardness of him between her legs was distracting, and somehow destroyed the magic of her breast sacrifice. (pp. 40–1)

Candy's imagery is frequently maternal, and she is often frustrated in her well-intentioned gestures. When the gardener begins to pummel her tiny clitoris 'with his calloused fingers', Candy fights down 'the desire to seize his hand, thinking how this was the price of loveliness and the key to the beautiful thrilling privilege of giving fully' (p. 41). Giving but not taking is the key to Candy's martyred sexuality.

With the extraordinary double penetration at the end of the novel by the holy man and the nose of Buddha's statue, Candy finally resolves her passive–active dilemma. When she is meditating on the tip of Buddha's nose, she realizes something wonderful:

all her life it had always been *she* who had been needed by someone else – mostly boys – and now at last she had found someone that she herself needed . . . Buddha! And yet, because of her early orientation, of always being the needed one (except by Daddy!), there was something vaguely dissatisfying and incomplete about it. If only the Buddha needed her! But she knew of course that this was a silly feeling and would in time be overcome. (p. 219)

After the great storm, in which the temple is struck by lightning, Candy has her final spiritual/sexual revelation. As the wetted and lubricated tip of the Buddha's nose gracefully eases itself into Candy's 'coyly arched tooky', she becomes aware, 'with the same lightning force of miracle which had split the roof, that wonder of wonders, *the Buddha, too, needed her!*' (p. 222) With this new knowledge Candy, 'with a sigh of indulgence', 'gave herself up fully to her idol' at the rear, whose ministrations provoke the holy man in front to achieve an equally miraculous orgasm. Thus Candy ends the book fully persuaded that she is needed by both Buddha and Daddy in simultaneous and perfect union. It is holy incest.

Only once in the novel does Candy experience orgasm: in the scene with the hunchback in Chapter 10. There is a total lack of comprehension between them, as Candy soliloquizes in her outlandishly purple and aesthetic prose of sophisticated benevolence, while the hunchback – christened Derek by Candy – indulges his freaky, subhuman, masturbatory fantasies. Candy apparently interrupts him while he is masturbating by rubbing his hump vigorously against a tree on Grove Street in Greenwich Village as he contemplates a store with men's underwear in the window. ' *"Rubatubdub!"* he said' (p. 132), which is his unique word for sex. ' "Three men in a tub!" cried Candy, laughing in marvel at their immediate rapport. How simple! she thought. How wonderfully, beautifully simple the important things are!' (p. 132). Candy is an early flower child, Zen-crazed and yearning to understand the deeper meanings that must lie behind appearances:

> She heard a wisdom and complex symbology in the hunchback's simple phrases. It was as though she were behind the scenes of something like the Dadaist movement, even creatively a part of it. This was the way things happened, she thought, the really big things, things that ten years later change the course of history, just this way, on the street corners of the Village; and here she was, a part of it. (p. 134)

Thus she needs the hunchback desperately as her entrée into the real world of life and art.

Meanwhile the hunchback is represented as a disgusting pervert, whose mind is 'filled with freakish thoughts. From an emotional standpoint, he would rather have been in the men's room down at Jack's Bar on the Bowery, eating a piece of urine-soaked bread' (p. 137). But Candy insists on giving herself with all the sophistication of the slick scenes in magazine fiction. She offers the obligatory onion omelet with tarragon and garlic, plus espresso, Camembert 'not too *bien fait*' (p. 139), a large bottle of Chianti, while she puts some Gregorian chants on the phono and offers Derek '*PR* [*Partisan Review*] and *Furioso*' (p. 136). All the cultural clichés are securely in place, as Candy does her provocative and almost misplaced striptease. '*I want to fuck you!*' (p. 141), says Derek, thinking in the back of his mind how he can rob Candy of her money. When Candy hesitates, the hunchback cunningly plays his trump card: ' "Is because of *this*?" he demanded. "Because of *this*?" He was sitting there with a wretched expression on his face, and one arm raised and curled behind his head, pointing at his hump' (p. 141). This fully turns Candy on, and, after a series of sadomasochistic preliminaries, she shrieks out with a wild impulsive cry – and pun: '*Give me your hump!*' (p. 149).

In Candy's mounting sexual excitement, she becomes transformed into a demonic, Dionysiac, frenzied creature, much like the hunchback himself. With a parodic inversion of birth, Derek

> lunged headlong toward her, burying his hump between Candy's legs as she hunched wildly, pulling open her little labias in an absurd effort to get it in her.
> 'Your hump! Your hump!' she kept crying, scratching and clawing at it now. (p. 149)

As she reaches orgasm, Candy explodes in a torrent of vicious invective: ' "Fuck! Shit! Piss!" she screamed. "Cunt! Cock! Crap! Prick! Kike! Nigger! Wop! *Hump*! HUMP!" and she teetered on the blazing peak of pure madness for an instant' (p. 149). For one redeeming moment, Candy can speak in the free style of Bubbles Girardi in *Portnoy's Complaint*. It is a moment of truth in the novel, but it is only a moment. The heroine quickly retreats to her web-spinning and soporific benevolence, full of the rhetoric of a New School course in the aesthetic sensibility.

Candy is always the sweet, wholesome, freshly scrubbed, peaches and cream, perfectly adorable, all-American girl. She was born on Valentine's Day and 'there *was* something like a Valentine about Candy – one of the expensive ones, all frills and lace, and fragrance of lavender' (p. 12). As she prepares for her visit to Professor Mephesto, Candy is very conscious of her appearance: 'Thank goodness for that at least, that she was wearing one of her smartest blouses, fresh and sweet, with her most lavishly embroidered slip peeking over the top through the V-neck, or V-breast, one might say, it being rather low' (p. 18). Candy is most consistently described as 'sweet': she is sweet, innocent and doll-like.

Southern and Hoffenberg lavish a good deal of attention on Candy's clothes. As she prepares to don the simple Cracker shift, Candy takes off the damp clothes of her former existence: ' "These prissy little panties are still wet!" she said, squeezing them into a tiny ball and giving them a kiss,' and she deposits her bundle of clothes with the receptionist: ' "Here," she said, "I *won't* be needing *these*! Give them to someone ... to some very *old* person" ' (p. 172). Candy's vanity is unbounded as she admires herself in the 'formless sackcloth shift with three buttons at the top': 'She loved the simple garment. It must have been such a garb as this, she reflected, that Joan of Arc had worn to her execution. She began to feel quite like a saint' (p. 172). Candy feels good about herself, very aware of the figure she cuts. There is a certain fastidiousness in her insistence on propriety in the most inflamed circumstances. After the gynecological incident in the men's room of the Riviera bar, when the police are taking her away in a squad car, Candy carries her skirt and panties in a dripping ball and refuses indignantly to put on wet clothes: ' "Good Night!" said Candy, "my things are soaking wet! How can I put *these on*?" ' (p. 163). A little later, however, Candy exclaims: 'I'm putting on my things, wet or not! Good Grief!' (p. 165). But they are distinctly 'icky' (p. 166). Candy always remains a perfect, comic-strip child. She learns nothing from her experiences, she never grows up and she continues to see the world with childlike wonder and its appropriate vocabulary.

Southern and Hoffenberg make a special point of describing Candy's genitalia in the arch and prettified language of early adolescence. Her cunt is a poeticized and highly euphemized attraction. It is the damp (p. 40), the sweet damp (p. 143), the sweetening damp (p. 62), the honeypot (p. 90), the fabulous honeypot (p. 144), the pink honeypot (p. 206), the precious little honey-cloister (p. 208), little honey-pouch (p. 214), precious and open honeypot (p. 221), sugar-scoop (p. 191), seething thermal pudding (p. 206), ever-sweetening pudding-pie (p. 221) and sweet-dripping little fur-pie (p. 205). Her teeny piping clitoris (p. 148) is primarily a piece of candy: it is the pink candy clit with slick lips all sugar and glue (p. 146), a sweet pink clit (p. 160), the pink pearl clit (p. 202) with pink-sugar walls (p. 208). Candy's perfect thing (p. 203) is the magnificent little jewel (p. 202), a marvelous little spice-box (p. 200), a pulsing jelly box (p. 95), a golden V (p. 95), an adorable pubes (p. 102) with darling little labia (p. 159) and rose-petal labia (p. 202). In other moods, it is snapping-turtle puss (p. 214) and the mysterious lamb-pit (p. 93), fabulous lamb-pit (p. 202) and tight little lamb-pit (p. 221). This is an extraordinary sexual lexicon with which to render Candy's delicious, delightful and precious attraction. She is an irresistible pop-art poster in bright, primary colors.

Candy is a masterful parody of middlebrow sentimentality in all its forms, and especially the romantic, wish-fulfillment, soft-core pornography that fills the pages of the popular women's magazines. Candy's bizarre relation to Dr Irving Krankeit, the Jewish psychiatrist ministering to her damaged Daddy, is pure soap opera in its evocation of sweetly titillating thoughts about a Mysterious Stranger who is suddenly understood to be Mr Right. Candy knows how to read the emotional symbolism of Daily Life:

> She wondered, couldn't this striding along together of theirs be a symbol of all that was to come? In the bright triumphs of his medical career, and also in the moments of anguish and doubt when it seemed to him that all his efforts were to end in ignominious failure – she would be at his side, marching along, as at present, to the next encounter with the Enemy, and lending him the soft assuring warmth of her femininity.

Candy Krankeit, she thought with a bittersweet thrill – so that was how it was to be! (p. 104)

Candy's reveries turn out to be immensely practical, as she prepares to snare her doctor – and not only a doctor, but a specialist! The only missing piece in the puzzle is the darling doctor himself:

> This fact, that Krankeit was still unaware of their loom-ing, destined love, only endeared him to her the more. The poor darling ninny, she thought, little did he realize the stark, aching need he had for her. She almost laughed aloud thinking of this obtuseness of his – so like a man too. (p. 105)

Dr Krankeit's stark, aching needs seem to lie in the area of acupuncture and masturbation, although Candy can hardly be expected to realize this. And Irving is also guarded by his mother, Mrs Sylvia Semite, who pretends to be a cleaning woman in the hospital in order to protect her marriageable Jewish boy. To her, Candy is a sex-crazed, buccaneering *shikse* who wants to snare an over-eligible Jewish husband. Sylvia Semite out-Portnoys the redoubtable Mrs Portnoy in her martyred and incestuous devotion to her son, and the prowling Candy is easily scared off. Southern and Hoffen-berg show an absolute genius in their deployment of cul-tural clichés, which float the outrageous sexuality. Candy's whorishness is displaced by her warmly benevolent feelings. So long as your heart is in the right place, everything is permitted to you, and Candy is the most right-thinking nymphomaniac in modern literature.

Working backwards, Vladimir Nabokov's *Lolita*, published by the Olympia Press in Paris in 1955, may be one of the models for *Candy*, published by the same press in 1958, just as *Candy* seems to lie behind *Blue Skies, No Candy*. All are novels preoccupied with sex and popular culture, or, to put it another way, they are novels that link sexual expression with other aspects of a consumerist society: sex is part of a histrionic, self-conscious, hedonistic and performative attitude. Kate, Candy and Lolita all use sex as a way of defining their social roles; their needs and the needs of others come together, so that they are simultaneously giving and taking. Sex is not an end in itself, but a way of proving your autonomy, and all three heroines have a natural genius for sex in all of its complex ramifications. None is even remotely a feminist, since the women assume meaning, sexually, only in relation to men and male values. All three establish a remarkably double perspective of participant and observer, naive and sophisticated, innocent and corrupt, sincere and ironic. These paradoxes underscore the idea of sex as performance, sex as theater, because the actor is acutely aware of his role.

Nabokov's concept of the nymphet is founded on the idea of doubleness. She is the early adolescent girl with hints and intimations of womanhood, but neither fully girl nor woman. She is pubescent and prepubescent at the same time, developed and undeveloped, at the turn of the tide, but definitely ripening toward something which has not yet been fulfilled. She represents expectancy and promise, but also a withering vulgarity. Nabokov tries to define his nymphet with the precision of a naturalist:

> Between the age limits of nine and fourteen there occur maidens who, to certain bewitched travelers, twice or many times older than they, reveal their true nature which is not human, but nymphic (that is, demoniac); and these chosen creatures I propose to designate as 'nymphets'. (p. 18)

To Humbert Humbert, speaking in his own defense at his murder trial, the nymphet is overwhelmingly a demonic creature, whose 'fey grace, the elusive, shifty, soul-shattering, insidious charm', separates her sharply from other girls. To the aging nympholept, she is defined as an aesthetic sex object:

> You have to be an artist and a madman, a creature of infinite melancholy, with a bubble of hot poison in your

loins and a super-voluptuous flame permanently aglow in your subtle spine (oh, how you have to cringe and hide!), in order to discern at once, by ineffable signs – the slightly feline outline of a cheekbone, the slenderness of a downy limb, and other indices which despair and shame and tears of tenderness forbid me to tabulate – the little deadly demon among the wholesome children; *she* stands unrecognized by them and unconscious herself of her fantastic power. (p. 19)

Nabokov evokes a folktale notion of the demon child, a Victorian *enfant maudit*, who is only partly human and who seeks, unconsciously of course, to return to that spirit world from which it has come. Such children are usually incredibly beautiful, but distant, cold, unfeeling, amoral, cruel and perhaps even psychopathic. Their demonic quality does not survive childhood, and they tend to die young and under mysterious circumstances, as the demon world claims its own. The children in Henry James's story, *The Turn of the Screw*, have qualities in common with Nabokov's nymphets, who most closely resemble the children in Edward Gorey's drawings – he would be the perfect illustrator for *Lolita*.

A nymphet must be demonic in order to deploy her incredible attraction. The idea of spiritual possession is important, because the nymphet is unaware of her insidious charm. Her demonic spirit endows her with a twofold nature, a mixture

of tender dreamy childishness and a kind of eerie vulgarity, stemming from the snub-nosed cuteness of ads and magazine pictures, from the blurry pinkness of adolescent maidservants in the Old Country (smelling of crushed daisies and sweat); and from very young harlots disguised as children in provincial brothels; and then again, all this gets mixed up with the exquisite stainless tenderness seeping through the musk and the mud, through the dirt and the death, oh God, oh God. (p. 46)

The nymphet, of course, only exists in the mind of the beholder, who defines her deadly attraction. It is he who is spiritually enthralled and whose demonic possession needs to be exorcised.

Nabokov is trying to describe the paradox of human sexuality, both bestial and angelic, in the profoundly ambivalent attitudes that Lolita arouses in her Humbert Humbert:

> A combination of naïveté and deception, of charm and vulgarity, of blue skies and rosy mirth, Lolita, when she chose, could be a most exasperating brat. I was not really quite prepared for her fits of disorganized boredom, intense and vehement griping, her sprawling, droopy, dopey-eyed style, and what is called goofing off – a kind of diffused clowning which she thought was tough in a boyish hoodlum way. Mentally, I found her to be a disgustingly conventional little girl. (pp. 149–50)

Nabokov's English is dazzling but not always responsive to American idiom, as in 'goofing off', an Army expression for shirking assigned duties, which takes on a new life in Nabokov's context. He seems to be confusing 'goofing off' with acting 'goofy', or nutty and clownish.

The real Lolita is ironically counterpointed against the fey Lolita who has taken possession of Humbert Humbert's soul. She it is

> to whom ads were dedicated: the ideal consumer, the subject and object of every foul poster. And she attempted – unsuccessfully – to patronize only those restaurants where the holy spirit of Huncan Dines had descended upon the cute paper napkins and cottage-cheese-crested salads. (p. 150)

As the 'ideal consumer', Lolita is a connoisseur of sex, and she reincarnates that dazzling Old World image of 'young harlots disguised as children in provincial brothels' (p. 46). It is the disguise and the doubleness that energize the ever-vigilant Humbert Humbert:

> Owing perhaps to constant amorous exercise, she radi-

ated, despite her very childish appearance, some special languorous glow which threw garage fellows, hotel pages, vacationists, goons in luxurious cars, maroon morons near blued pools, into fits of concupiscence which might have tickled my pride, had it not incensed my jealousy. (p. 161)

Nabokov's style endows Humbert Humbert with a certain stilted unreality. His sexual obsession is rendered chiefly by his obsession with language rather than by the kind of minute erotic description one finds in *My Secret Life*. And Nabokov's language is a strangely synthetic and displaced American lingo. Thus 'garage fellows' is a phrase without any colloquial meaning, and it appears to be translating something literally from either German or Russian. We may also note that there are no 'pages' in American hotels, only 'bellhops' or 'bellboys'. I suspect that there is at least one error in American idiom on every page of *Lolita*, so that Nabokov's language seems a made-up, syncretistic language of the imagination. Just as Lolita seems a creature of Humbert Humbert's inflamed and tumescent fancy, so does Nabokov's American English seem an aesthetic artifact, with daring excursions into a macaronic slang translated from the leading European languages.

It is essential for the novel that Lolita be conceived as a little madonna/whore. As in Freud's essay, 'The most prevalent form of degradation in erotic life', which figures so importantly in *Portnoy's Complaint*, the sex object must be degraded in order to be sexual and elevated in order to be loved. These two currents endow sexuality with its intensely paradoxical nature. The lack of resolution enhances the guilty pleasure with which our whorish madonna is violated. Before we meet Lolita, we have already encountered Monique, the Parisian prostitute whom Humbert Humbert engages near the Madeleine:

She came hardly up to my chest hair and had the kind of dimpled round little face French girls so often have, and I liked her long lashes and tight-fitting tailored dress sheathing in pearl-gray her young body which still retained – and that was the nymphic echo, the chill of delight, the leap in my loins – a childish something mingling with the professional *frétillement* [waggling] of her small agile rump. (p. 23)

Monique's petite, delicate, girl-like physique evokes the 'nymphic echo'. It is very specifically physical, and Nabokov supplies abundant details. She has a 'compact, neat, curiously immature body'. After shedding her clothes 'with fascinating rapidity', she listens 'with infantile pleasure' to an organ-grinder in the courtyard below. 'With her brown bobbed hair, luminous gray eyes and pale skin, she looked perfectly charming. Her hips were no bigger than those of a squatting lad' (p. 24). She is a nymphet because her sexuality is ambiguous and not fully defined; she is a girl/woman and a girl/boy. She is both innocent and vulgarly professional: 'a delinquent nymphet shining through the matter-of-fact young whore' (p. 25).

The archetypal nymphet in *Lolita* is the 'girl-child' Annabel, whom Humbert Humbert, himself a child, wooed on the Riviera. The fervid, awkward and unconsummated passion occurs in this Poe-like 'kingdom by the sea': 'When I was a child and she was a child . . . ' (p. 19) Nabokov cunningly places his first love in the allusive context of Poe's poem, 'Annabel Lee', and he must surely have been aware of Poe's own penchant for nymphets like his 13-year-old bride/cousin, Virginia Clemm. In Poe's essay, 'The philosophy of composition' (1846), he declares that there is no more poetic topic than the death of a beautiful woman. Poe's Annabel Lee is the model for Nabokov's frail and fated Annabel, whose passion is 'dreamy and eerie . . . half-pleasure, half-pain' (p. 16). Deprived of a consummation that is tantalizingly near, Humbert Humbert will yearningly try to re-create the moment: 'But that mimosa grove – the haze of stars, the tingle, the flame, the honey-dew, and the ache remained with me, and that little girl with her seaside limbs and ardent tongue haunted me ever since' (p. 17).

'Honey-dew', we remember, is the food of Coleridge's enchanted 'Kubla Khan': 'For he on honey-dew hath fed/ And drunk the milk of Paradise' – presumably a narcotic like laudanum.

To pursue the knotted web of allusion, 'haze' is Lolita's family name, and when Humbert Humbert first sees her he has the shock of *déjà vu*.

> there was my Riviera love peering at me over dark glasses.
>
> It was the same child – the same frail, honey-hued shoulders, the same silky supple bare back, the same chestnut head of hair. . . . And, as if I were the fairy-tale nurse of some little princess (lost, kidnaped, discovered in gypsy rags through which her nakedness smiled at the king and his hounds), I recognized the tiny dark-brown mole on her side. . . . The twenty-five years I have lived since then, tapered to a palpitating point, and vanished.
> (p. 41)

Annabel is re-created in a Proustian flood of memory images, including 'those puerile hips on which I had kissed the crenulated imprint left by the band of her shorts' (p. 41). Why crenulated? Because Annabel/Lolita is a work of art, and a work of art is supremely a creation of the imagination, and Nabokov's imagination bathes in the benthic depths of language, which transforms the gross materials of the real world into the eroticized, reified images of a reality that exists only in the mind of the perceiver. Humbert Humbert's language is not only artful, but also self-consciously artificial. Leaves and shells are crenulated if they have tiny notches, scallops or grooves, but the elastic waistband of a girl's underwear can only create crenulations by poetic license. Humbert Humbert is in love with Annabel/Lolita insofar as she can be re-created in words, and Nabokov practises a self-regarding eroticism very much in the style of William Gass' philosophical inquiry, *On Being Blue* (see Introduction, p. 10).

After Lolita escapes with her lover, Humbert Humbert

pursues them in the company of Rita, a mock-nymphet twice Lolita's age:

> The oddly prepubescent curve of her back, her ricey skin, her slow languorous colombine kisses kept me from mischief. It is not the artistic aptitudes that are secondary sexual characters as some shams and shamans have said; it is the other way around: sex is but the ancilla of art. (p. 261)

This describes not only the style of *Lolita*, but its basic attitude to sex. Sex is the handmaiden of art and not its master. Art comes first, which uses sex for its own imaginative purposes. Art creates sex, defying biology and the secondary sexual characteristics. Humbert Humbert is an artist who uses sex as his subject and material; that is his only form of creativity. The demonic nymphets are his inspiration. They have no autonomous artistic being outside the mind of their creator. As surely as the imprisoned Marquis de Sade spun out his masturbatory fantasies, Humbert Humbert peoples a forbidden, fairy-tale world with golden girls he himself has endowed with life. His own sexual consummation therefore has little or nothing to do with the unworthy subjects on which it so dearly depends.

Humbert Humbert also creates a grotesque and kitsch America as the stage-set for his erotic adventures. This, too, is a country of the mind, very much in the spirit of Portnoy's inflamed declaration: 'through fucking I will discover America' (p. 235). In a revealing afterpiece at the end of the novel, 'On a book entitled *Lolita*', Nabokov explains how he 'invented' America, with connotations of the Latin sense of 'discover': 'I needed a certain exhilarating milieu. Nothing is more exhilarating than philistine vulgarity' (p. 317). The 'philistine vulgarity' of America mirrors a corresponding vulgarity in Humbert Humbert and his Lolita. He sees a reality congenial to his own perverse imagination, which projects a zany America distorted by the funhouse mirror of the mind:

> Obvious Arizona, pueblo dwellings, aboriginal picto-

graphs, a dinosaur track in a desert canyon, printed there thirty million years ago, when I was a child. . . . A winery in California, with a church built in the shape of a wine barrel. . . . Somber Yellowstone Park and its colored hot springs, baby geysers, rainbows of bubbling mud – symbols of my passion. . . . A zoo in Indiana where a large troop of monkeys lived on concrete replica of Christopher Columbus' flagship. (pp. 159–60)

This is pure kitsch and camp, a reality imitating bad works of art, seedy and third-class.

Humbert Humbert's America is intensely Europeanized, so that it is always being compared with some unstated original in Switzerland, France or pre-revolutionary Russia. Nabokov is constantly floating in remembrances of 'the splendid Hotel Mirana' on the French Riviera, owned by the father of Humbert Humbert and which revolves around him 'as a kind of private universe, a whitewashed cosmos within the blue greater one that blazed outside' (p. 12). If the protagonist's America is sordid and tawdry, so is his infatuation with Lolita: both are set against more refulgent scenes and persons (Annabel) in the past.

There is a consistent irony running between past and present. Humbert Humbert and Lolita eat in roadside restaurants suitably furnished to mirror their kitschy passion:

from the lowly Eat with its deer head (dark trace of long tear at inner canthus), 'humorous' picture post cards of the posterior 'Kurort' ['spa' in German] type, impaled guest checks, life savers, sunglasses, adman visions of celestial sundaes, one half of a chocolate cake under glass, and several horribly experienced flies zigzagging over the sticky sugar-pour on the ignoble counter; and all the way to the expensive place with the subdued lights, preposterously poor table linen, inept waiters (ex-convicts or college boys), the roan back of a screen actress, the sable eyebrows of her male of the moment, and an orchestra of zoot-suiters with trumpets. (p. 157)

This is in the satirical/apocalyptic, end-of-the-world style of Nathaniel West's *Day of the Locust* (1939). It is so vividly depicted that it becomes a surrealistic nightmare.

We may conclude with a simple inventory of objects Humbert Humbert buys for Lolita as they begin their long odyssey across the United States:

> In the gay town of Lepingville I bought her four books of comics, a box of candy, a box of sanitary pads, two cokes, a manicure set, a travel clock with a luminous dial, a ring with a real topaz, a tennis racket, roller skates with white high shoes, field glasses, a portable radio set, chewing gum, a transparent raincoat, sunglasses, some more garments – swooners, shorts, all kinds of summer frocks. (pp. 143–4)

This list tells us all we need to know about the seething sexual imagination of Humbert Humbert. In his mad and heroic attempt to unite the real world with the frenzied delights of his sexual imagination, he is doomed to ignominious failure:

> There she would be, a typical kid picking her nose while engrossed in the lighter sections of a newspaper, as indifferent to my ecstasy as if it were something she had sat upon, a shoe, a doll, the handle of a tennis racket, and was too indolent to remove. (p. 167)

Humbert Humbert cannot grapple with the consumerist culture in which he is fated to find his bliss. In this world everything is equivocal, and our protagonist tries to persuade himself of his tainted happiness:

> Despite our tiffs, despite her nastiness, despite all the fuss and faces she made, and the vulgarity, and the danger, and the horrible hopelessness of it all, I still dwelled deep in my elected paradise – a paradise whose skies were the color of hell-flames – but still a paradise. (p. 168)

This is surely a satanic vision of paradise, a mirage, an illusion, an ecstasy that is an act of faith that cannot be realized in the phenomenological world. Nabokov is toying with our deepest sexual fantasies, which are mocking and evanescent. If Humbert Humbert sounds like a latter-day Whitman in his erotic inventory of America, in his vision America is also a crazy wasteland of sexual narcissism. Finally, 'sex is but the ancilla of art', which alone can give this nightmare form and meaning.

8 CONCLUSION

AFTER so many pages of discussion, the complex nature of sexual fiction still eludes us. We need to be constantly reminded that we are dealing with words on the printed page and not with sexuality itself as a biological function. The words must be very potent – consider the tremendous force of censorship, especially in the *Lady Chatterley's Lover* case in America and England. Many reputable witnesses for the prosecution testified that Lawrence's words did indeed have the power to deprave and corrupt. This is surely a proof of Lawrence's success in arousing his readers. Most books can hardly engage their audience to read them from beginning to end. Once we are aware that it is only words on the printed page, sexual fiction is removed from the area of carnal temptation too powerful to resist. We read of our own free will, and no society, however well meaning, can legislate for our imagined good in literature and against our imagined depravation.

If our only commerce was with the classics – and culture could conceivably be restricted to the exact five feet of the Harvard Classics bookshelf – we would be in a sorry state indeed for understanding the turbulent life around us. We read for a variety of reasons, not the least of which is to deepen our perceptions about ourselves. Surely sexual fiction can be justified in this psychological and humanistic area. It is only partly a wish-fulfillment, fantasy literature. Some vital part of it is concerned with obsessions, with provocative but unconscious motivations, with our troubled relation to our childhood and our parents, and with a crushing boredom and the impulse both to transcendence and to self-annihilation. No matter how disturbing it is to read the Marquis de Sade, for example, he does succeed in calling us back to our primitive urges and away from the patina of overcivilized acceptance which is the surface of our lives. In his intense nihilism, Sade is a reflective author.

The scope of *Sexual Fiction* has been limited to sexually explicit books in the mainstream of English, American and European literature. Not all are acclaimed masterpieces, even of sexual writing, but they all represent attitudes or positions essential for our discussion. We have tried to explore the subject in a topographical way, testing the limits of sexuality as a theme at various ends of the spectrum between banality and excessive, ideational abstraction. At its worst, sexual fiction is preprogrammed and prepackaged according to popular formulas; at its best, it is moving, teasing, provocative, cathartic and transcendent. We are challenged to confront our secret selves in all of our splendor and degradation.

Some readers might object that real erotica in green covers or plain brown-paper wrappers and sold for adults only in adult-type bookstores does not figure at all in this book. Despite the powerful arguments of Michael Perkins in *The Secret Record*, a detailed account of the popular erotic literature of the 1960s and 1970s, I am not convinced that any of his authors I have been able to read merits inclusion in the present study. Perhaps further reading will make me a convert to the full backlist of Olympia Press and Essex House. On the other side, I had similar difficulties with soft-core pornography along the lines of Harold Robbins, *The Adventurers*, and Jacqueline Susann's *Valley of the Dolls*, both so conveniently published in 1966. These books are only intermittently sexual and intermittently violent (and often intermittently sexual *and* violent together). They are not consistently sexual narratives. This is a romantic, wish-fulfillment literature, where sex is not central but only spices a novel that is really about power in society, how to achieve it and how to keep it.

I have also decided not to take up the rich sexual literature that is specifically homosexual or lesbian; that definitely requires a separate study. Although Sade, Pauline Réage and Jean de Berg use homosexual and lesbian themes, as does *My Secret Life*, their overt emphasis is heterosexual. Despite points of comparability, straight and gay authors seem to be talking about a sexual experience that is fundamentally different. For Jean Genet, for example, who figures so importantly in Kate Millett's *Sexual Politics*, we would need different criteria to deal with the interplay of sexuality and narcissism in his works. Erotic violence in Genet is not the same thing as the sadomasochistic games in Sade. In sum, I do not believe that there is a single, comprehensive eroticism that can include all sexual literature in one single entity.

Much more remains to be written about the differences between male and female perceptions of sexuality. For one thing, we need a much larger and more autonomous body of sexual writing by women and addressed to specific aspects of the feminine experience. If it is true that literature is created out of other literature – out of conventions and models and genre assumptions – then women have only a male literature on which to base their own attempts at a distinctive form of female sexual expression. Unfortunately, sexual fiction has more or less defined itself historically as a specifically male genre. It will take a great deal of productivity to break this historical mold, although novels like *Fear of Flying* and *Blue Skies, No Candy* seem already to be accomplishing something perceivably different.

Despite the fact that sexual fiction is created primarily by males and with masculine values, the overwhelming interest in these books is in the representation of female sexuality. This is the central mystery. Is it the product of an oedipal striving to understand and master our earliest anxieties, especially in relation to our mothers? Mrs Portnoy and Sylvia Semite (in *Candy*) emerge with a forbidding vitality as we see them involved in a heroic struggle to overprotect and

symbolically to castrate their respective Alexanders and Irv-
ings. Perhaps the intensely voyeuristic quality of sexual literature, most notably in *My Secret Life*, expresses traumatic
feelings about the primal scene. The psychoanalytic under-
pinnings of sexual fiction would make a fascinating topic for
further exploration along the lines of Freud's essay, 'The
most prevalent form of degradation in erotic life', which is
profoundly relevant to the sexual motives of characters in
fiction. It is obvious that the deeper and more covert the
sexual fears lie, the more they energize the fiction in which
they are involved.

It is paradoxical that male sexuality is everywhere so
vaguely and so unsatisfactorily represented. It is as if the
predominantly male authors were suppressing the other
side of the equation. Lawrence, for example, seems positively afraid of Mellors, the gamekeeper, who is a pretty
ungenerous, churlish and vain malcontent. What about
male vulnerability, especially the fact that the male sexual
organs are blatantly exposed and easily subject to evaluation
(limp or stiff) and castratory injury? Erica Jong has some
acute insights about Adrian's 'limp prick', that 'penetrated
where a stiff one would never have reached' (p. 90). Perhaps
we need female authors to tell us about male sexuality, and
that is the new topic that will define an emerging, characteristically female sexual fiction. For men, their own sexuality arouses too much anxiety to be successfully represented.

Humor is one of the safety valves in sexual fiction. Portnoy's frenzied imaginings are perceived in a therapeutic
context and are therefore amusingly honest. He shares all of
his worst fears with the reader. He is awkward, self-
conscious, haunted by guilt to such an extent that we can
safely laugh with him and feel an enormous sympathy for
his anxieties. Similarly, Humbert Humbert in *Lolita* wins
our grotesque sympathy for his bizarre sexual adventures
that are also intensely narcissistic and innocent. The laughter is both a form of release and a mode of celebration.
When Candy reaches orgasm with her hunchback Derek,
she explodes in a flood of vicious invective that has an

unaccustomed ring of truth in a book that is all parodic disguise. As readers, we want to laugh at the sex scenes to assuage our own guilty anxieties about being involved, even vicariously, in the lurid events we are reading. Laughter is a way of breaking an empathy that has grown too strong. We need some of that alienation effect that Brecht tried to introduce into his plays.

Sex as a literary subject matter has certain inherent difficulties. Its physical aspects are extremely limited, so that one is naturally diverted from direct description to the cluster of feelings and perceptions associated with the experience. Direct description of orgasm, for example, produces the synthetically rapturous and poetized vocabulary of Lawrence's *Lady Chatterley's Lover,* which is hardly direct at all. Walter's physiological details in *My Secret Life* are also unsatisfying because so painfully limited; there is no sense at all in this book of a spontaneous joyousness produced by sexual union. Perhaps Cleland had the right idea in *Fanny Hill* when he chose to show us orgasm as a triumph of hyperbolic and poetically euphemized language. The dirty words that Cleland avoids would only depress us. Sex in Cleland is primarily a work of art, a product of the imagination, as it is in Nabokov's *Lolita*. By abandoning any pretense at exact description, the authors do nevertheless capture the emotional tone of orgasm, whose intensity is comically rendered.

The question of repetition in sexual literature keeps coming up without there being any satisfying way of answering it. A strong sense of concentrated detachment is one of the characteristic products of sexual themes. There is a certain fascination in this kind of reverie, which is radically different from boredom, where one just simply stops reading and does something else. Sexuality is most frequently represented as an unconscious and involuntary compulsion which drives the characters almost against their wills. This obsessive quality is important for literature. Walter's satyriasis in *My Secret Life* is the driving force of the book, so that we have a series of sexual adventures that resemble each other but which occur in a sequence that builds up to something larger than any single event. We anticipate the next experience from the previous one, and, as readers, we seem to be caught in a compulsive forward movement similar to Walter's. At its best, his life in the book becomes our life. In Sade's *Justine* we also move in an almost predictable course, but the repetition tends to intensify the action. Admittedly, it is a book that could go on forever or end at any point, but it needs to have a certain magnitude in order to create the right effect. We couldn't imagine *Justine* as a short book.

Sexual fiction demands a concentration of effect, an intensity that can only be produced by the hypnotic sense of a world apart. Like Macbeth, we are 'rapt' – attentive, alert, ready, preoccupied – but for only one kind of experience. There is a narrowing of focus by which we are caught up in the narrative process. At its best, sexual fiction demands a special kind of alertness by which we participate in the enactment of a powerful fantasy. In 'The pornographic imagination', Susan Sontag has some provocative remarks about the natural affinity between science fiction and erotic writing. 'Pornography is one of the branches of literature – science fiction is another – aiming at disorientation, at psychic dislocation.' In both, 'The physical sensations involuntarily produced in the reader carry with them something that touches upon the reader's whole experience of his humanity – and his limits as a personality and as a body' (p. 191). Its sexual stimulation is a form of 'proselytizing', since all products of the pornographic imagination are characterized by 'their energy and their absolutism' (p. 207). Absolutism very vividly describes the effect of a reader's being possessed by the book he is reading. This intense and physical engagement of the imagination is true of sexual fiction at its best.

I could, of course, have written *Sexual Fiction* with an entirely different set of sexual books. The examples are not so important as the ideas and attitudes involved. I believe that sexual fiction is a definable subject and a perceivable

kind of literature, with assumptions, conventions and limitations of its own. We have been considering how the sexual
subject matter in some way predetermines the kinds of
things that can be done with it. It seems to me crucial that
sexual fiction should not be studied apart from literature in
general. What makes *Lady Chatterley's Lover* moving is not
essentially different from what makes *Sons and Lovers* and
Women in Love moving. There is nothing special in the sexual
theme that can conceivably set *Lady Chatterley's Lover* apart.
Although *Story of O* is openly erotic – no one needs to dispute
this, even for legal purposes – it is also a profoundly disturbing philosophical fable. The sexual apparatus borrowed
from Sade and sadomasochistic literature is the means by
which themes of slavery and freedom are projected.

This distinction is well developed by Harry Levin in his
attack on censorship in 'The unbanning of the books':

> If we abandon censorship, we depend all the more
> imperatively upon criticism. If we agree that books are
> neither dirty nor clean, we must be sure to remember that
> they are bad or good, and must not be distracted into
> ignoring that difference. After all, it has never been too
> difficult to tell a potboiler from a work of art, and it
> should be even simpler with potboilers that concentrate
> upon sex to the point of monotony. To criticize them is to
> discriminate between artistic imagination and autistic
> fantasy. (p. 81)

Sexual fiction does not have its own sexual criticism, so that
the subject matter neither advantages nor disadvantages the
genre. That is a point of fundamental importance.

It is, nevertheless, obvious that authors of sexual fiction
begin with tremendous advantages. They can appeal to the
reader's own psyche more directly than, let us say, authors
of detective novels. Our experience of murder is surely
more remote than our experience of sexuality. The removal
of censorship in most of its forms provides a tremendous
opportunity for writers of sexual fiction. They no longer
need to titillate readers with the promise of forbidden

scenes. They can now openly use a sexual subject matter for the exploration of the most profound experience. Sex is so deeply invested with feeling in our culture that it is an admirable vehicle to convey insights of the most searing kind of truth. Sexual fiction could resurrect the novel as a vital and lively form, because sexuality is capable of providing convincing images of life. Our sexual fiction needs no apology. If it is not always attractive, it is at least always true.

BIBLIOGRAPHY

Critical works (and collections of essays) of special significance are starred (*).

ANONYMOUS, *My Secret Life*, abridged with an introduction by G. Legman (New York: Grove Press, 1966).

ANONYMOUS, *My Secret Life*, unabridged (Secaucus, N.J.: Castle Books, 1967).

ATKINS, JOHN, *Sex in Literature: The Erotic Impulse in Literature* (New York: Grove Press, 1972).

*BARTHES, ROLAND, *Sade Fourier Loyola*, trans. Richard Miller (New York: Hill and Wang, 1976).

BARZUN, JACQUES, 'Venus at large: sexuality and the limits of literature', *Encounter*, 26 (1966), 24–30.

BASLER, ROY, *Sex, Symbolism, and Psychology in Literature* (1948) (New York: Octagon Books, 1967).

*BATAILLE, GEORGES, *Death and Sensuality: A Study of Eroticism and the Taboo* (New York: Ballantine Books, 1969).

*BEAUVOIR, SIMONE DE, *The Marquis de Sade, with Selections from His Writings Chosen by Paul Dinnage* (New York: Grove Press, 1954).

BERG, JEAN DE, *The Image* (1956), trans. Patsy Southgate (New York: Grove Press, 1967).

*BERSANI, LEO, *A Future for Astyanax: Character and Desire in Literature* (Boston: Little, Brown, 1976).

BRECHER, EDWARD M., *The Sex Researchers* (Boston: Little, Brown, 1969).

BRECHER, EDWARD and RUTH (eds), *An Analysis of Human Sexual Response* (New York: New American Library, 1966).

BROWN, NORMAN O., *Love's Body* (New York: Random House, 1966).

BROWNMILLER, SUSAN, *Against Our Will: Men, Women and Rape* (New York: Bantam Books, 1976).

BRUCE, LENNY, *How to Talk Dirty and Influence People* (Chicago: Playboy Press, 1967).

*BUCHEN, IRVING (ed.), *The Perverse Imagination: Sexuality and Literary Culture* (New York: New York University Press, 1970).

CALVERTON, V. F., and S. D. SCHMALHAUSEN (eds), *Sex in Civilization* (Garden City, N.Y.: Garden City Publishing Co., 1929).

*CARTER, ANGELA, *The Sadeian Woman and the Ideology of Pornography* (New York: Harper & Row, 1980).

CLELAND, JOHN, *Memoirs of a Woman of Pleasure* (1749) (New York: Putnam, 1963). Also popularly called *Fanny Hill.*

COHEN, JOHN (ed.), *The Essential Lenny Bruce* (New York: Ballantine Books, 1967).

COMFORT, ALEX, *The Joy of Sex* (New York: Simon & Schuster, 1974).

DAVENPORT, GUY, 'The dawn in Erewhon', *Tatlin!* (New York: Scribner's, 1974), 131–261.

*DEFORGES, RÉGINE, *Confessions of O: Conversations with Pauline Réage*, trans. Sabine d'Estrée (New York: Viking/Seaver, 1979).

DI LAURO, AL, and GERALD RABKIN, *Dirty Movies: An Illustrated History of the Stag Film 1915–1970* (New York: Chelsea House, 1976).

EDWARDES, ALLEN, *The Jewel in the Lotus: A Historical Survey of the Sexual Culture of the East* (New York: Bantam Books, 1976).

ELSOM, JOHN, *Erotic Theatre* (New York: Dell, 1973).

FIEDLER, LESLIE A., *Love and Death in the American Novel* (Cleveland: World, 1962).

*FISHER, SEYMOUR, *The Female Orgasm: Psychology, Physiology, Fantasy* (New York: Basic Books, 1973).

*—— *Understanding the Female Orgasm* (New York: Basic Books, 1973).

FLIEGEL, ZENIA ODES, 'Feminine psychosexual development in Freudian theory: a historical reconstruction', *Psychoanalytic Quarterly*, 42 (1973), 385–408.

*FOUCAULT, MICHEL, *The History of Sexuality, Vol. I: An Introduction*, trans. Robert Hurley (New York: Pantheon, 1978).

FOXON, DAVID, *Libertine Literature in England 1660–1745* (New Hyde Park, N.Y.: University Books, 1965).

*FREUD, SIGMUND, 'The most prevalent form of degradation in erotic life' (1912), trans. Joan Rivière, in Benjamin Nelson (ed.), *On Creativity and the Unconscious* (New York: Harper & Row, 1958), 173–86.

*—— *Three Contributions to the Theory of Sex*, in *The Basic Writings of Sigmund Freud*, trans. and ed. A. A. Brill (New York: Modern Library, 1938).

FRIDAY, NANCY, *Forbidden Flowers: More Women's Sexual Fantasies* (New York: Pocket Books, 1975).

—— *Men in Love: Men's Sexual Fantasies: The Triumph of Love Over Rage* (New York: Delacorte, 1980).

—— *My Secret Garden: Women's Sexual Fantasies* (New York: Pocket Books, 1974).

*GASS, WILLIAM, *On Being Blue: A Philosophical Inquiry* (Boston: Godine, 1975).

GILL, BRENDAN, 'Blue notes', *Film Comment*, Jan.–Feb. 1973.

GINZBURG, RALPH, *An Unhurried View of Erotica* (New York: Helmsman Press, 1958).

GIRARD, RENÉ, *Deceit, Desire, and the Novel: Self and Other in Literary Structure*, trans. Yvonne Freccero (Baltimore: Johns Hopkins University Press, 1965).

GIRODIAS, MAURICE, 'The erotic society', *Encounter*, 25 (1965), 52–8.

—— (ed.), *The Olympia Reader: Selections from the Traveller's Companion Series* (New York: Black Watch, 1965).

GLICKSBERG, CHARLES I., *The Sexual Revolution in Modern American Literature* (The Hague: Nijhoff, 1971).

—— *The Sexual Revolution in Modern English Literature* (The Hague: Nijhoff, 1973).

GOLDFARB, RUSSELL M., *Sexual Repression and Victorian*

Literature (Lewisburg, Pa: Bucknell University Press, 1970).

GORER, GEOFFREY, 'The Marquis de Sade', *Encounter*, 18 (1962), 72–8.

—— 'The pornography of death', *Encounter*, 5 (1955), 49–52.

GREENE, GAEL, *Blue Skies, No Candy* (New York: Warner, 1976).

GREER, GERMAINE, *The Female Eunuch* (New York: Bantam Books, 1972).

HAGSTRUM, JEAN H., *Sex and Sensibility: Ideal and Erotic Love from Milton to Mozart* (Chicago: University of Chicago Press, 1980).

HARRIS, FRANK, *My Life and Loves* (1923–7), John F. Gallagher (ed.) (New York: Grove Press, n.d.).

HERNTON, CALVIN C., *Sex and Racism in America* (New York: Grove Press, 1965).

*HITE, SHERE, *The Hite Report: A Nationwide Study on Female Sexuality* (New York: Macmillan, 1976).

*HUGHES, DOUGLAS A. (ed.), *Perspectives on Pornography* (New York: St Martin's Press, 1970).

HYDE, H. MONTGOMERY, *A History of Pornography* (New York: Dell, 1966).

JONG, ERICA, *Fanny* (New York: New American Library, 1980).

—— *Fear of Flying* (New York: New American Library, 1974).

—— *How to Save Your Own Life* (New York: New American Library, 1978).

KAPLAN, ABRAHAM, 'Obscenity as an esthetic category', *Law and Contemporary Problems*, 20 (1955), 544–59. Part of a symposium, Obscenity and the Arts, in this issue. Reprinted in Rist (see p.176).

KINSEY, ALFRED C., *et al.*, *Sexual Behavior in the Human Female* (Philadelphia: Saunders, 1953).

—— *Sexual Behavior in the Human Male* (Philadelphia: Saunders, 1948).

KOTZWINKLE, WILLIAM, *Nightbook* (New York: Avon, 1974).

KRASH, ABE, review of *The Trial of Lady Chatterley*, C. H. Rolph (ed.), in *Yale Law Journal*, 71 (1962), 1351–63.

KRONHAUSEN, PHYLLIS and EBERHARD, *Erotic Fantasies: A Study of the Sexual Imagination* (New York: Grove Press, 1970).

—— *Pornography and the Law: The Psychology of Erotic Realism and Pornography* (New York: Ballantine Books, 1959).

LAWRENCE, D. H., *Etruscan Places* (1932) (New York: Viking, 1957).

—— *Lady Chatterley's Lover* (1928) (New York: New American Library, 1959).

*—— *Sex, Literature, and Censorship*, Harry T. Moore (ed.) (New York: Viking, 1959).

LEGMAN, G., *The Horn Book: Studies in Erotic Folklore and Bibliography* (New Hyde Park, N.Y.: University Books, 1964).

—— *Rationale of the Dirty Joke: An Analysis of Sexual Humor*, First Series (New York: Grove Press, 1971).

—— *Rationale of the Dirty Joke: An Analysis of Sexual Humor*, Second Series (New York: Bell, 1975).

LÉLY, GILBERT, *The Marquis de Sade a Biography*, trans. Alec Brown (New York: Grove Press, 1962).

*LEVIN, HARRY, 'The unbanning of the books', *Atlantic Monthly*, 217 (1966), 77–81. Reprinted in Levin, *Refractions: Essays in Comparative Literature* (New York: Oxford University Press, 1966), 296–307, and in Hughes.

LIPTON, LAWRENCE, *The Erotic Revolution: An Affirmative View of the New Morality* (Los Angeles: Sherbourne Press, 1965).

LOTH, DAVID, *The Erotic in Literature* (New York: Macfadden, 1962).

McCONNACHIE, BRIAN (ed.), *The Job of Sex: A Workingman's Guide to Productive Lovemaking* (New York: Warner, 1974). *National Lampoon* parody.

MAILER, NORMAN, *An American Dream* (New York: Dial, 1965).

—— 'Henry Miller: genius and lust, narcissism', *American Review*, 24 (1976), 1–40.

—— *The Prisoner of Sex* (Boston: Little, Brown, 1971). A

reply to Kate Millett's attack in *Sexual Politics*.

*MARCUS, STEVEN, *The Other Victorians: A Study of Sexuality and Pornography in Mid-Nineteenth Century England* (London: Corgi, 1969).

MASTERS, WILLIAM H., and VIRGINIA E. JOHNSON, *Human Sexual Response* (Boston: Little, Brown, 1966).

*MASTERS, WILLIAM H., and VIRGINIA E. JOHNSON in association with Robert J. Levin, *The Pleasure Bond: A New Look at Sexuality and Commitment* (Boston: Little, Brown, 1974).

MICHELSON, PETER, *The Aesthetics of Pornography* (New York: Herder & Herder, 1971).

MILLER, HENRY, 'The apocalyptic Lawrence', *Southwest Review*, 31 (1946), 254–6.

—— *Black Spring* (1936) (New York: Grove Press, 1963).

—— *Quiet Days in Clichy* (1956) (New York: Grove Press, 1965).

—— *The Rosy Crucifixion: Sexus* (1962), *Plexus* (1963), and *Nexus* (1960), 3 vols. (New York: Grove Press, 1965).

—— *Tropic of Cancer* (1934) (New York: Grove Press, 1961).

—— *Tropic of Capricorn* (1939) (New York: Grove Press, 1961).

—— *The World of Sex* (New York: Grove Press, 1965).

*MILLETT, KATE, *Sexual Politics* (Garden City, N.Y.: Doubleday, 1970).

*MITCHELL, EDWARD (ed.), *Henry Miller: Three Decades of Criticism* (New York: New York University Press, 1971).

MORAWSKI, STEFAN, 'Art and obscenity', *Journal of Aesthetics and Art Criticism*, 26 (1967), 193–207.

NABOKOV, VLADIMIR, *Lolita* (1955) (New York: Putnam, n.d.).

NIN, ANAIS, *Delta of Venus* (New York: Bantam Books, 1978).

—— *Little Birds* (New York: Bantam Books, 1979).

NOBILE, PHILIP (ed.), *The New Eroticism: Theories, Vogues and Canons* (New York: Random House, 1970).

*ORWELL, GEORGE, 'Inside the whale' (1940), in Mitchell, *Henry Miller*, 7–25.

*PECKHAM, MORSE, *Art & Pornography: An Experiment in Explanation* (New York: Basic Books, 1969).

*PERKINS, MICHAEL, *The Secret Record: Modern Erotic Literature* (New York: Morrow, 1976).

PIETROPINTO, ANTHONY, and JACQUELINE SIMENAUER, *Beyond the Male Myth: What Women Want to Know about Men's Sexuality* (New York: New American Library, 1978).

*POLSKY, NED, 'On the sociology of pornography', *Hustlers, Beats, and Others* (Chicago: Aldine, 1967), 186–202.

POROSKY, P. H., (ed.), *The Erotic Anthology* (New York: New American Library, 1972).

READE, BRIAN (ed.), *Sexual Heretics: Male Homosexuality in English Literature from 1850 to 1900* (New York: Coward-McCann, 1971).

RÉAGE, PAULINE, *Return to the Château* (1969), preceded by *A Girl in Love*, trans. Sabine d'Estrée (New York: Grove Press, 1973).

—— *Story of O* (1954), trans. Sabine d'Estrée (New York: Grove Press, 1965).

REMBAR, CHARLES, *The End of Obscenity* (New York: Random House, 1968).

REUBEN, DAVID, *Everything you always wanted to know about sex but were afraid to ask* (New York: Bantam Books, 1971).

RIST, RAY C., (ed.), *The Pornography Controversy* (New Brunswick, N.J.: Transaction Books, 1975).

ROLPH, C. H. (ed.), *Does Pornography Matter?* (London: Routledge & Kegan Paul, 1961).

ROTH, PHILIP, *Portnoy's Complaint* (New York: Random House, 1969).

ROUGEMONT, DENIS DE, *Love Declared: Essays on the Myths of Love*, trans. Richard Howard (New York: Pantheon, 1963).

—— *Love in the Western World*, trans. Montgomery Belgion (New York: Pantheon, 1956).

SADE, MARQUIS DE, *Juliette*, trans. Austryn Wainhouse (New York: Grove Press, 1968).

—— *Justine, Philosophy in the Bedroom and Other Writings*, trans. Richard Seaver and Austryn Wainhouse (New York: Grove Press, 1966).

—— *The 120 Days of Sodom and Other Writings*, trans. Austryn

Wainhouse and Richard Seaver (New York: Grove Press, 1967).

SEAMAN, BARBARA, *Free and Female* (Greenwich, Conn.: Fawcett Books, 1973).

*SHERFEY, MARY JANE, *The Nature and Evolution of Female Sexuality* (New York: Random House, 1972).

*SONTAG, SUSAN, 'The pornographic imagination', *Partisan Review,* 34 (1967), 181–212. Reprinted in Sontag, *Styles of Radical Will* (New York: Farrar, Straus & Giroux, 1969), 33–73, and in Hughes.

SOUTHERN, TERRY, *Blue Movie* (New York: New American Library, 1971).

SOUTHERN, TERRY and MASON HOFFENBERG, *Candy* (1958) (New York: Putnam, 1964).

STEINER, GEORGE, 'Night words: high pornography and human privacy', *Encounter,* 25 (1965), 14–19. Reprinted in Steiner, *Language and Silence* (New York: Atheneum, 1967), and in Hughes, Nobile and Rist. See also the *Encounter* articles by Girodias and Barzun.

*STOEHR, TAYLOR, 'Pornography, masturbation and the novel', *Salmagundi,* 2 (1966), 28–56.

STOLLER, ROBERT J., *Perversion: The Erotic Form of Hatred* (New York: Pantheon Books, 1975).

—— *Sex and Gender, Volume I: The Development of Masculinity and Femininity* (New York: Jason Aronson, 1974).

*WALLING, WILLIAM, '*Candy* in context', in Maurice Charney (ed.), *Comedy: New Perspectives, New York Literary Forum,* 1 (1978), 229–40.

WALTERS, RONALD G., *Primers for Prudery: Sexual Advice to Victorian America* (Englewood Cliffs, N.J.: Prentice-Hall, 1974).

WINSTON, MATHEW, '*Lolita* and the dangers of fiction', *Twentieth Century Literature,* 21 (1975), 421–7.

WITTIG, MONIQUE, *Les Guérillères,* trans. David Le Vay (New York: Avon Books, 1973).

Yale French Studies, 35 (1965). Issue devoted to Sade.

YOUNG, WAYLAND, *Eros Denied: Sex in Western Society* (New York: Grove Press, 1964).

INDEX